# Signed, Healed, Delivered: Testimonies of the Supernatural Power of God

## By: Dr. Rebecca Burgess

# Signed, HEALED, DELIVERED

*Healed,
Restored,
Delivered.*

*Testimonies of the*
**Supernatural Power of God**

## DR. REBECCA BURGESS

# PRAISE FOR SIGNED, HEALED, DELIVERED

Dr. Rebecca Burgess shares her personal experiences - as well as personal challenges - and how they have enhanced and grown her relationship with God. The testimonies she shares allow readers to see how her faith in God and His faithfulness have brought her through the most challenging moments of her life. Readers will be encouraged and enriched by not only the stories, but the teachings throughout her book that you can apply to your life today.

**Mrs. Debra A. Williams, Author**
**Christian Educator, 1st Lady - Shiloh Baptist Church**

# DEDICATION

To Jesus Christ, my Savior and Redeemer—thank You for giving me new life and turning my testimony into a message of hope. This book belongs to You.

To my husband, Keith A. Burgess, and to our children—this book is for you. Your love, encouragement and belief in me have given me the strength to press forward, even in the hardest seasons. I thank God for each of you.

To my father, Hazrat A. Lalmohamed—thank you for the values you instilled in me that laid the foundation for every success I have achieved. You are the best father, and this book is dedicated to you.

This work is dedicated with love and gratitude to each of you.

# CONTENTS

# INTRODUCTION
## The Power of Testimony in Jesus

**Revelation 12:11**
*"And they overcame him by the blood of the Lamb, and by the word of their testimony; and they loved not their lives unto the death."*

A testimony is more than just a recounting of events; it is a declaration of God's faithfulness, power and grace in the life of an individual. It is a beacon of hope, shining light into the hearts of others, reminding them that the same God who brought you through the fire can do the same for them.

A testimony reveals the intersection of human brokenness and divine restoration. It speaks of battles fought and victories won, not by our strength but through the limitless love and mercy of a Savior who never leaves nor forsakes us. It is a living proof that no pit is too deep for God to rescue, no heart too shattered for Him to heal, and no sin too great for Him to forgive.

When shared, a testimony becomes a seed of faith for others, a reminder that their story is still being written by the Author of life. It declares that God's promises are true, His timing perfect, and His purposes unshakable. In essence, a testimony isn't just about what happened to us; it's about who God is—faithful, powerful and unchanging.

"Signed, Healed, Delivered" is more than a title. It is a declaration of transformation, hope, and divine purpose. This book is a journey through the remarkable ways God's presence can transform lives, bringing healing to the broken, freedom to the bound, and purpose to those who feel lost.

For years, I wrestled with challenges that felt insurmountable. I experienced seasons of pain, doubt and uncertainty, but in those moments, I discovered that God's power to restore is unmatched. Like a signature that authenticates a document, God's hand was evident in my life—affirming my worth, claiming me as His own, and directing my path.

Through His grace, I found healing—not just in my physical body, but in the deepest parts of my heart and soul. Wounds I thought would never close became testimonies of God's restorative power. What once seemed like irreversible brokenness became opportunities for growth and renewal.

God led me into freedom, equipping me to live boldly and purposefully. The journey was not easy, but every step revealed His faithfulness.

This book is for those who feel unseen, unheard or unworthy. It's for anyone seeking hope in the midst of despair, healing in the face of brokenness, or freedom from the things that hold them captive. Through personal stories, scriptural truths, and practical reflections, my prayer is that "Signed, Healed & Delivered" will encourage and inspire you to trust in the transformative power of God.

To be "signed in Christ" means belonging to Him and identifying with His name. Just as a signature represents ownership or authorship, being "signed" by Christ reflects that believers are His. A signature is often a symbol of finality or validation. Being "signed in Christ" reflects the assurance that salvation is secure because it is authored and guaranteed by Jesus.

Being healed in Christ is a profound experience of restoration that touches every aspect of our being—spirit, soul and body. It begins with the forgiveness of sin, where the broken relationship between humanity and God is reconciled through Jesus' sacrifice on the cross. This spiritual healing transforms us into new creations, freeing us from guilt, shame, and the power of sin. In Christ, we also find emotional healing as He binds up the wounds of our hearts, bringing peace to our fears and comfort in our sorrows. Physical healing is another dimension, as Jesus demonstrated His authority over sickness and disease, while offering hope and renewal even in the face of physical challenges. Ultimately, healing in Christ points us to the promise of eternity, where pain and suffering will be no more. To be healed in Christ is to embrace the wholeness and freedom found in His love, power and presence, trusting Him to make all things new in His perfect time.

Being delivered in Christ means experiencing the power of Jesus to set us free from the chains of sin, fear and oppression. Through His death and resurrection, Jesus broke the power of darkness and declared victory over anything that seeks to bind or enslave us. Deliverance in Christ is not just a momentary event but an ongoing process of walking in freedom and victory, guided by His truth and Spirit. In a Christian context, being delivered refers to being set free from spiritual bondage, oppression, or any stronghold that hinders one's relationship with God. It often means being rescued by Jesus Christ from sin, demonic influence, addiction, fear, sickness, generational curses, or any form of spiritual captivity. Deliverance is a demonstration of God's power to break chains and bring wholeness to a person's life. As we place our faith in Him, He delivers us from the grip of the enemy and transfers us into His kingdom of light, where we can live in purpose, peace and authority. To be delivered in Christ is to walk boldly in the freedom He purchased for us, knowing that "if the Son sets you free, you will be free indeed." (John 8:36)

Being signed by God and sealed by the Holy Spirit means allowing Jesus Christ to take full ownership of our lives. Many of us are broken, hurting, and in desperate need of healing. If we remain bound by chains of sin, pain, and unresolved wounds, we cannot function as God intended or be vessels to help others. Chains of addiction, bitterness, fear or unforgiveness weigh us down, keeping us from walking in freedom. But Jesus came to heal the brokenhearted and set the captives free. Until we surrender fully to Him—allowing His healing power to restore us and His Spirit to empower us—we will remain stagnant, unable to move forward in purpose or fulfill the call on our lives. Only by being signed, healed and delivered can we truly rise to walk in victory and serve others in love.

Each chapter is filled with declarations because they are powerful. The Bible reminds us in Proverbs 18:21 (KJV) that "Death and life are in the power of the tongue: and they that love it shall eat the fruit thereof." What we speak has the ability to shape our reality, to either build us up or tear us down. So don't skip over these declarations. Speak them aloud, with faith and conviction, knowing that your words carry weight. Repeat them multiple times until you believe them, until they take root in your heart and mind. These declarations are not just empty words—they are seeds planted in your spirit, and in due season, they will bear fruit. Don't just say them once and move on; keep declaring them until the truth of God's promises manifests in your life. You have the authority to speak life into your circumstances, and as you do, you will see transformation.

As you turn these pages, may you find the courage to step into your own story of being signed, healed and delivered. May you discover that no matter where you've been or what you've endured, God's grace is sufficient, His love is endless, and His power is more than enough.

This is not just my testimony, it is a testament to what is possible for anyone who dares to trust God completely. Welcome to the journey.

# Testimony #1
# Barren to Bearing Fruit

**Isaiah 54:1 KJV**

*Sing, O barren, thou that didst not bear; break forth into singing, and cry aloud, thou that didst not travail with child: for more are the children of the desolate than the children of the married wife, saith the LORD.*

My story began long before I ever existed, crafted by divine hands and written in the heavens. My mother, a woman of unwavering faith, was barren for the first five years of her marriage. The doctors gave their opinions, and although the whispers of doubt came from many directions, my parents never stopped believing. They chose prayer over panic, faith over fear. My mom was a prayer warrior, unshaken by the impossible, holding tightly to the promises of God.

For five years, she and my father prayed fervently. The world would call it persistence. They called it trust. They believed in a God who hears, who sees, and who answers. In the stillness of one of those long nights of waiting, my mother had a dream. In that dream, God revealed to her she would conceive a daughter and her name would be Rebecca.

When she awoke, her spirit was filled with hope. The dream was not just a promise; it was a glimpse of what was to come. Not long after, the impossible became possible—my mom became pregnant. True to the dream, I was born, and they named me Rebecca, as God had ordained. Every detail and every step of my journey was already written. The devil tried to stop my existence, but he could not. And just as he could not stop me, he cannot stop you.

You were created with purpose, formed with intention, and born with destiny. Maybe the enemy tried to block your existence because your very life is a threat to him. But his plans can never outmatch the Creator's will.

So, as you read this, know this truth: your presence here is no accident. The same God who brought me into being has done the same for you. You are not only chosen—you are necessary.

**Physically Barren, Powerfully Healed**

Physical barrenness refers to the inability to conceive or bear children due to biological factors. This can stem from various medical conditions, such as infertility in women, hormonal imbalances, blocked fallopian tubes, or polycystic ovary syndrome (PCOS). In men, it may be caused by low sperm count, poor motility, or other reproductive challenges. Beyond the physical aspects, barrenness often carries a deep emotional and psychological burden. Many individuals or couples wrestle with feelings of inadequacy, grief and frustration, particularly in societies where having children is viewed as a mark of fulfillment and success.

However, barrenness is not always just a biological issue—it can also have a spiritual dimension. In some cases, demonic influences, generational curses, or unseen spiritual barriers may contribute to infertility or hinder the process of conception. The enemy seeks to delay or destroy the fruitfulness that God has destined for His children, using barrenness as a tool to bring despair and doubt.

Many times, when faced with barrenness, we turn inward and place the blame on ourselves. We wonder if it is because we waited too long to marry or did not choose the "right" partner. We carry the weight of regret, shame and self-blame, believing our choices are the sole reason for our struggles. Yet, we often fail to recognize that many factors—both physical and spiritual—are beyond our control. True healing and breakthrough come when we surrender to God, seek His wisdom, and trust in His divine timing and power to bring forth life, whether physically or through the many other ways He blesses His children.

I remember experiencing a powerful deliverance when demonic spirits manifested, revealing that they did not want me to marry or have children. These forces sought to block the very blessings God had ordained for my life. However, God, in His infinite wisdom, also revealed this attack to my apostle, who stood in prayer and spiritual warfare on my behalf. Through God's power, the chains were broken, and both blessings—marriage and children—came to pass.

This experience was a testament to the authority of Jesus Christ over every demonic assignment and the power of prayer in securing victory. In later chapters, I will delve deeper into this journey, sharing the battles I faced, the spiritual principles I learned, and the faithfulness of God in bringing His promises to fulfillment.

**Biblical Accounts of Barrenness and God's Intervention**

The Bible offers powerful stories of hope and divine intervention, reminding us that God is not only aware of our struggles but is also able to bring restoration and healing.

The Scriptures are replete with stories of women who faced barrenness and experienced God's miraculous power in their lives. These accounts provide encouragement and assurance that God sees, hears and cares deeply for His daughters.

1. **Sarah**: Sarah, the wife of Abraham, waited decades for the fulfillment of God's promise to make Abraham a father of nations. Despite her initial doubts and laughter at the idea of bearing a child in old age, God's word was fulfilled when Isaac was born (Genesis 21:1-7). Sarah's story reminds us that God's timing is perfect and His promises never fail.
2. **Hannah**: Hannah's longing for a child drove her to fervent prayer, pouring out her heart before God in the temple. Her faith and perseverance were rewarded when God blessed her with Samuel, who became a great prophet (1 Samuel 1:10-20). Hannah's story highlights the power of prayer and unwavering trust in God.
3. **Elizabeth**: In the New Testament, Elizabeth, the mother of John the Baptist, experienced barrenness well into her old age. Yet, her faithfulness and righteousness were honored by God, who blessed her with a son destined to prepare the way for the Messiah (Luke 1:5-25). Elizabeth's story illustrates that God's plans are far greater than we can imagine.

If God healed Sarah, Hannah, and Elizabeth from barrenness, He can do it for you as well. The same God who opened their wombs is still a miracle-working God today.

If you are struggling with barrenness, take heart. The same God who moved in their lives is able to move in yours. What seems impossible in the natural is possible with God (Luke 1:37). He sees your pain, hears your prayers, and is able to bring life where there has been emptiness. Trust in His timing, stand on His promises, and believe that He who did it before can do it again.

## Understanding Barrenness Beyond the Physical

While barrenness often refers to the physical inability to conceive, it can also symbolize spiritual or emotional desolation. Women and men may feel barren in other areas of life—dreams unfulfilled, relationships broken, or a sense of purposelessness. These forms of barrenness can be equally painful, but the same God who heals physical barrenness is able to bring renewal and fruitfulness to every barren place in our lives. Spiritual barrenness is a lack of growth, productivity and connection with God. It is a season where life feels unfruitful and stagnant. But even in times of barrenness, God is calling us to be fruitful and multiply—not just in the physical sense, but spiritually as well. Being fruitful means using our talents, skills and resources to glorify God and fulfill His purpose for us.

Through barrenness, there is no life; it is a state of non-existence. The enemy desires for you to remain in that state, to feel invisible and unproductive, for he does not want you to be fruitful and multiply—physically or spiritually. Just as the sperm must meet the egg to conceive, we must meet with God to conceive the promises He has for us. Mary conceived through the Holy Spirit because she was highly favored, chosen by God to carry and give birth to the Savior. When you align with God's will and live in obedience to His calling, you become a vessel through which His plans for your life can be birthed, bringing forth life and fruitfulness.

Barrenness can feel like a shut door, one that seems impossible to open no matter how hard you try. It may appear locked by circumstances, unfulfilled desires, or years of waiting. However, just like any locked door, there is a key—and that key is faith in God. In Christ, the key to unlocking barrenness is trusting in His power, His promises, and His perfect timing. No matter how tightly the door may seem sealed, God holds the authority to open it, bringing life, restoration, and breakthrough. Through prayer, faith, and surrender, the closed door of barrenness can be opened, allowing God's fruitfulness to enter and transform every area of your life.

Barrenness is often a tool that Satan uses to try to keep you locked out from the fullness of God's purpose for your life. He seeks to sow doubt, discouragement, and hopelessness, trying to convince you that you are not worthy or that God's promises are not for you. By keeping you focused on what appears to be a closed door, he aims to distract you from the truth that God has a plan and a purpose for your life that is far greater than your current circumstances. But in Christ, we have the authority to reject the enemy's lies and claim the promises of God. No matter how long the struggle with barrenness may last, it is not the final word. God's purpose for you cannot be thwarted, and He is faithful to unlock the doors that Satan tries to keep closed, bringing you into His destiny for your life.

Barrenness can be seen as a demonic spirit that seeks to rob individuals of their God-given purpose, joy, and the blessings of fruitfulness. It is a spiritual stronghold that manifests in both physical and emotional forms, hindering the ability to conceive or experience growth in various areas of life. This spirit works to instill feelings of inadequacy, shame, and hopelessness, causing one to believe he or she is incapable of receiving the promises of God. However, in the name of Jesus, this demonic spirit can be cast out. Through the authority given to us by Christ, we can break the power of barrenness and declare life, restoration and fruitfulness. Just as Jesus cast out demons and healed the sick, we too can stand in faith, command every spirit of barrenness to leave, and receive the fullness of God's blessings and purpose for our lives.

**Moving from Barrenness to Fruitfulness**

God desires to move us from a state of spiritual barrenness to a life of fruitfulness. While this can include physical fruitfulness, such as having children, it also involves spiritual productivity—living a life that glorifies God, growing in faith, and using our God-given gifts to impact the world. Just as physical conception requires intimacy, spiritual fruitfulness also begins with intimacy with God. We must spend time in His presence to conceive His plans and purposes for our lives.

**The Seed Matters!**

STOP! I repeat STOP engaging in spiritual intimacy with the wrong partner! Many people make the mistake of choosing the wrong person to be intimate with, sometimes even having children, only to regret it later. We often wonder why we are spiritually barren, but the truth lies in the choices we make. When we choose the wrong partner, we align ourselves with destruction instead of purpose. By being intimate with Satan rather than God, we allow seeds of anger, rage, bitterness, and unforgiveness to take root in our lives. Satan's desire is for us to fail, to never fulfill our God-given purpose. The seed matters—who are you receiving your seed from? Whatever seed you nurture will grow. If you are intimate with Satan, you will produce things that lead to death and stagnation. However, intimacy with God brings life. He transforms barrenness into fruitfulness, allowing you to give birth to the destiny He has prepared for you. Satan represents death, causing dreams and potential to die before they even begin. But God represents life, bringing forth purpose and abundance. Choose wisely who you align with. Your future depends on it.

I remember witnessing countless people at my church come in burdened with barrenness, both physical and spiritual. Their longing for breakthrough was evident, and their faith unwavering as they sought prayer and trusted God for a miracle. They would receive a prophetic word spoken over their lives—"Go and prepare." That simple yet profound command reminded them that faith requires action. It was not enough to just hear the word. They needed to align their actions with their belief. They stepped out in faith, preparing their hearts and homes, trusting that God would fulfill His promise.

Time after time, they would return to the church filled with joy, testifying of God's miraculous power. God had healed their wombs, and they were now carrying the promise they had prayed for. It was a beautiful reminder that faith without works is dead. When God speaks, we must move—acting on His word with expectation, knowing that He is faithful to perform what He has promised. Their testimonies were not only a demonstration of God's healing power but also a reminder that when we align our actions with His word, miracles happen, and barrenness is turned into fruitfulness. This transformation happened when they chose to make God their intimate partner.

**The Virgin Conceived**

Mary experienced a divine conception because she was intimately connected with the right partner—the Holy Spirit. In this supernatural union, the Holy Spirit overshadowed her, and through this holy intimacy, she conceived Jesus, the Son of God. This was a spiritual intimacy, not physical, highlighting the importance of being in alignment with God's Spirit to bring forth His purposes.

The fact that the Virgin Mary conceived Jesus may not make sense from a human perspective, but it was a divine miracle orchestrated by God. According to Luke 1:34-35 (KJV), when the angel Gabriel told Mary she would conceive a child, she responded, *"How shall this be, seeing I know not a man?"* She understood that conception typically required physical intimacy, yet the angel explained that the Holy Spirit would come upon her, and the power of the Most High would overshadow her. This supernatural event ensured Jesus was born not of human will, but by divine intervention—fully God and fully man, yet sinless.

This miraculous conception fulfilled the prophecy in Isaiah 7:14 - *"Therefore the Lord Himself shall give you a sign; Behold, a virgin shall conceive and bear a son and shall call His name Immanuel."* - and demonstrated that nothing is impossible for God (Luke 1:37). While it defied human logic, it was a divine act that made salvation possible for all mankind. Just as Mary's conception of Jesus was beyond natural comprehension, many of God's works surpass human reasoning. Faith calls us to trust that God can do the impossible—even when it does not make sense in the natural. God's promise to bring forth the Savior through a virgin is one of the most powerful examples of His ability to use the natural to reflect spiritual truths.

This reminds us that when God calls us to bring forth His purposes, it is not about our abilities but His power working through us. Mary's example teaches us to trust God even when His plans seem impossible by human standards.

**Birthing Process**

When God plants a vision, dream or purpose within us, it's like conception. But carrying that vision to full term and delivering it requires faith, perseverance and preparation.

**The Journey from Conception to Birth:**

1. **Conception:** God plants a dream or purpose within you.

2. **Carrying the Vision:** Just like a physical pregnancy, spiritual growth requires nurturing through prayer, faith, and trust in God.
3. **Labor:** This is the most intense part of the process, where challenges arise, but breakthrough is near.
4. **Delivery:** Bringing forth the vision God placed within you into the world.

Many dreams die before they are born because of doubt, fear, or external challenges. Yet, just as couples can try to conceive again, God is a God of second chances. He says, *"I am giving you another opportunity to carry this holy thing."* This time, protect it through prayer, speak life over it, and trust Him to bring it to fruition.

**Spiritual Preparation for Labor**

1. **Spiritual Prenatal Care:** Stay in the word of God and maintain a strong prayer life.
2. **Equip Yourself:** Learn from the Bible and teachings to navigate spiritual labor.
3. **Support System:** Surround yourself with people who will pray for and encourage you.
4. **Pack Your Spiritual Hospital Bag:** Carry Scriptures, prayer notes, and lessons to sustain you through labor.

**Labor - The Final Push**

Before a birth can take place, labor must come first. Just as natural childbirth is accompanied by contractions, pressure, and intense effort, spiritual labor involves its own signs, struggles and moments of travail. When God is about to birth something new in your life—whether it is a ministry, a breakthrough, a calling or a promise—there will often be resistance. You may face spiritual warfare, discouragement, or even moments of doubt. But just as contractions signal that delivery is near, these challenges often indicate something significant is about to come forth.

**That Baby Has to Come Forth**

When Mary gave birth to Jesus, she was not just delivering a child—she was bringing forth the fulfillment of prophecy. Matthew 1:23 (KJV) declares, *"Behold, a virgin shall be with child, and shall bring forth a son, and they shall call His name Emmanuel, which being interpreted is, God with us."* Her labor was not just physical but deeply spiritual, ushering in the greatest gift to mankind—God in the flesh. In the same way, when God places something inside of you, it is not meant to stay dormant. It must be birthed into the world.

**The Power of Naming**

After Mary gave birth, she named the child **Jesus**, as instructed by the angel (Luke 1:31). Naming is significant—it declares identity, purpose and destiny. Likewise, when God births something through you, you must recognize and name it. Whether it is a calling, a vision, a ministry, or a promise fulfilled, giving it a name is an act of faith. It signifies you acknowledge what God has done, and you are ready to walk in the fullness of His purpose.

So, push through the labor pains. The discomfort is only temporary, but the promise is eternal. What God has placed within you **must** come forth, and when it does, it will carry the name and purpose He has ordained.

**Trusting the Birthing Process**

Wherever you are in the journey—from barrenness to conception, preparation, or labor—trust God's process. He has placed something holy within you, and His grace will carry you through to delivery.

**Remember**

- Conception requires intimacy with God.
- Carrying the vision requires faith and perseverance.
- Labor may bring pain, but it leads to birth.
- Naming the purpose reflects its significance and destiny.

God is saying: *"Prepare, for you are about to go into labor."* The spiritual intersects with the natural, and what you have conceived will soon come into existence. Trust Him to bring it forth in His perfect timing, and be ready to declare the name of the promise He fulfills through you.

**Go Where You Can Safely Deliver**

When a woman goes into labor, she must go to the right place—a hospital or a birthing center—where the necessary equipment, support and expertise are available to ensure a safe delivery. Staying in the wrong environment, without the proper tools and care, can put both the mother and baby at risk. Likewise, when you are in spiritual labor—when God is birthing something new in your life—you must be in the right place, surrounded by the right people, under the right covering.

**Let Dr. Jesus Deliver You**

Some places and people are not equipped to handle the weight of what God is bringing forth in your life. Staying in environments that lack spiritual nourishment, faith, or godly guidance can delay or even hinder the birthing process. You need the presence of Dr. Jesus, the Great Physician, to guide you through the labor and ensure what He has placed inside of you is safely delivered.

Jesus knows exactly how to bring forth what He has planted within you. He has the wisdom, the power, and the perfect timing. So do not settle in a place where you are spiritually malnourished or unsupported. Go where you can grow. Go where you can deliver. Go where you can thrive. And most importantly, trust Dr. Jesus to ensure the purpose, vision and promises within you will come forth in His perfect way.

**You Are an Overcomer!**

Spiritual barrenness is a condition that can leave us feeling dry, disconnected and purposeless. It is a season where God may seem distant, prayers feel unanswered, and our spiritual vitality seems to wither. Yet, even in these times, God's promises hold true. He is the God who makes streams in the desert and causes life to flourish in barren places. Overcoming spiritual barrenness requires intentionality, faith, and the willingness to trust God in the process. Here are steps to help you navigate and triumph over this season.

**1. Acknowledge the Season**

The first step in overcoming spiritual barrenness is to recognize and acknowledge it. Denying your feelings or pretending everything is fine will only prolong the dryness. Be honest with yourself and with God. Reflect on questions like:

- When did I start feeling this way?
- Are there circumstances or choices contributing to this season?

Acknowledging spiritual barrenness is not a sign of weakness but an act of humility. It opens the door for God to begin His work of restoration.

Scripture for Reflection: *"Come unto me, all ye that labour and are heavy laden, and I will give you rest."* (Matthew 11:28 KJV)

## 2. Return to the Source

In seasons of barrenness, our connection to God—the true source of life—often needs renewal. Just as a plant cannot thrive without water, our spirits cannot flourish without intimacy with God. Return to Him through:

- **Prayer**: Even when it feels hard, pour out your heart to God. Honest, consistent prayer reopens the lines of communication.
- **Scripture**: God's Word is a wellspring of life. Meditate on passages that speak of His faithfulness and restoration.
- **Worship**: Worship shifts your focus from your dryness to God's greatness. It creates an atmosphere where His presence can dwell.

Scripture for Reflection: *"But whosoever drinketh of the water that I shall give him shall never thirst; but the water that I shall give him shall be in him a well of water springing up into everlasting life."* (John 4:14 KJV).

## 3. Remove Obstacles

Sometimes spiritual barrenness arises because of unaddressed sin, unforgiveness or distractions that pull us away from God. Take time to evaluate what might be hindering your spiritual growth. Ask yourself:

- Are there habits or behaviors I need to surrender?
- Is there someone I need to forgive?
- Have I allowed busyness or worldly pursuits to crowd out my time with God?

Repentance and surrender clear the path for God's renewal.

Scripture for Reflection: *"Wherefore seeing we also are compassed about with so great a cloud of witnesses, let us lay aside every weight, and the sin which doth so easily beset us, and let us run with patience the race that is set before us."* (Hebrews 12:1 KJV)

## 4. Seek Community

Isolation can exacerbate spiritual barrenness. God created us for community, and being surrounded by other believers provides encouragement and accountability. Seek out:

- A trusted mentor or spiritual leader who can pray with you and provide guidance.
- A small group or Bible study to share your struggles and find mutual support.
- Holy Ghost filled church gatherings to experience corporate worship and teaching.

Scripture for Reflection: *"Not forsaking the assembling of ourselves together, as the manner of some is; but exhorting one another: and so much the more, as ye see the day approaching."* (Hebrews 10:25 KJV)

## 5. Cultivate Gratitude

In seasons of barrenness, it is easy to focus on what feels lacking. Gratitude shifts our perspective and reminds us of God's past faithfulness. Keep a journal of blessings, even small ones, and thank God for them daily. Gratitude fosters hope and keeps your heart open to His work.

Scripture for Reflection: *"In everything give thanks: for this is the will of God in Christ Jesus concerning you."* (1 Thessalonians 5:18 KJV)

## 6. Embrace God's Timing

Overcoming spiritual barrenness does not happen overnight. Trust that God is working even when you cannot see it. Just as seeds take time to sprout, your spiritual renewal requires patience and faith in His perfect timing. Remain steadfast and continue to seek Him, knowing He is faithful to complete the work He started in you.

Scripture for Reflection: *"To everything there is a season, and a time to every purpose under the heaven."* (Ecclesiastes 3:1 KJV)

## 7. Prepare for the Bloom

Barrenness is not the end of your story. It is a season that God can use to refine you, deepen your faith, and prepare you for a greater harvest. Stay expectant and ready to embrace the new things God will bring forth in your life.

Scripture for Reflection: *"Behold, I will do a new thing; now it shall spring forth; shall ye not know it? I will even make a way in the wilderness, and rivers in the desert."* (Isaiah 43:19 KJV)

## Spirit of Barrenness

Demonic influence in the context of barrenness (infertility) is a topic often discussed within certain theological and Christian perspectives. Some individuals believe that spiritual forces or demonic influence can affect areas of life such as fertility, and they may interpret struggles with barrenness as being linked to spiritual attacks or demonic oppression.

Christians believe God has power over all things - including fertility - and infertility may occur for various reasons, such as biological, medical or spiritual causes. In some instances, spiritual warfare prayers or deliverance ministry might be recommended for those who believe demonic forces are hindering fertility.

However, it is important to approach this topic with discernment, compassion, and an understanding that medical, psychological and social factors also contribute to challenges related to infertility. Many would encourage prayer, seeking healing through faith, and also considering medical assistance when facing issues like barrenness.

If you discern that the spirit of barrenness is at work in your life, physically or spiritually, seek God wholeheartedly through prayer, fasting, and deliverance ministry. By addressing this spiritual hindrance with faith and action, you can break free from the cycle of unfruitfulness and step into the abundant life and blessings God has destined for you. With God's help, no area of your life is beyond His ability to restore and make fruitful.

Before casting out any spirit, it is important to repent for any personal or ancestral sin that may have opened the door for this spirit to take hold. This includes confessing any doubts, fears or resentment toward God and forgiving others, as unforgiveness can be a stronghold. Praying the word of God over your life is one of the most powerful ways to break spiritual barrenness. Declare God's promises over your situation, rebuking the spirit of barrenness in Jesus' name. Command the spirit to leave and renounce any spiritual hindrance or delay.

Sometimes, breaking the spirit of barrenness or any other stronghold in your life may require more than just personal prayer and effort. This is where seeking someone who specializes in deliverance becomes crucial. Deliverance is the act of removing spiritual oppression or demonic influences through prayer, the power of the Holy Spirit, and the authority of Jesus Christ.

**Message of Hope**

Are you struggling with the burden of barrenness? *"Sing, O barren"* is a powerful declaration that calls forth faith and expectation in the midst of barrenness. It is a command to rejoice and praise, even when the circumstances seem empty or unfruitful. In Isaiah 54:1, God instructs the barren woman to sing, not because she already sees the results, but because of the promise that is yet to be fulfilled. Singing in barrenness is an act of trust, acknowledging that even in the seasons of waiting and longing, God is at work. It is a declaration of hope, a proclamation that what seems impossible is possible with God. When you sing in your barrenness, you are declaring God's promises will not return void, and He is preparing you for the upcoming breakthrough. It is not the absence of pain or struggle, but the presence of faith that brings forth the fruitfulness He has ordained for your life.

It is time to give birth to your son or daughter. It is time to give birth to your God-given destiny. Just as a mother carries life within her and brings it forth in due season, God has placed purpose and destiny within you that is ready to be birthed. Now is the moment to step into the fullness of what He has called you to, to release the promises He has spoken over your life, and to see them come to fruition. The time for waiting is over. Your purpose is about to manifest, and the blessings God has prepared for you are ready to come forth. Trust in His timing and His power, for what He has placed inside of you is meant to change the world.

**Declaration**

I declare I am healed from both physical and spiritual barrenness. In Christ, I receive His abundant life, restoration and fruitfulness.

No matter the circumstances, I trust God's timing and His power to bring forth blessings from every area of my life. I believe He is turning my pain into purpose and filling me with His life-giving presence. I am not defined by limitations, but by the limitless power of God working in and through me. His promises are true, and I walk in the fullness of His healing and restoration. I declare that my physical and spiritual womb is open, and I will conceive. I trust in God's divine timing and power to bring forth His promises in my life. Just as He opened the wombs of Sarah, Hannah and Elizabeth, He is opening mine to receive His blessings, healing and purpose.

# Testimony #2
# Grief to Gratitude

**Matthew 5:4 KJV**
*"Blessed are they that mourn: for they shall be comforted."*

Tragedy struck my dad's and my life when I was just a child, too young to fully understand what was happening but old enough to feel the loss. My mother passed away when I was only two years old, just one week before my third birthday. She had been in the hospital, and though I was too little to grasp the gravity of the situation, I could sense the sorrow in the air.

Losing her was like a shadow falling over our lives—a moment that shifted everything. For my father, it was a devastating blow. For me, it was confusing. At that tender age, I did not fully understand death, but I knew something was missing.

It would have been the perfect moment to ask God, why. Why would He take her away? Why would He leave my father and me to navigate life without her? But even in my father's grief, he clung to the truth of God's word, *"For I know the plans I have for you,"* declares the LORD in Jeremiah 29:11. *"...Plans to prosper you and not to harm you, plans to give you hope and a future."*

My father sat me down and gently explained how my mother had gone to heaven. My little heart struggled to process the enormity of that reality. I looked up at him, wide-eyed, and asked, *"Can I go to children's heaven?"* It was my way of wanting to be where she was, my innocent yearning for a connection that seemed suddenly severed.

From that day on, my father stepped into a role he never imagined he would face so soon—a single parent. I commend him for the strength he showed during such a difficult time. Raising me without my mom was no small task. He was not perfect—no one is—but he did his best. He worked tirelessly to provide, nurture and guide me through the years, even while dealing with his own grief.

Over time, God began to heal both of us. We accepted that my mother had fulfilled her calling on this earth. She was a powerful woman of God who had left an indelible mark on everyone she encountered. She was a worshiper, an intercessor, and someone who boldly declared God's Word. Though her time here was brief, her legacy was eternal.

My dad made sure I was always surrounded by amazing, delicious food, especially his specialty—authentic Guyanese dishes I grew to love. He spoiled me in every way. From a young age, I was into fashion—clothes, shoes and jewelry—and he indulged me in it all. I was known as the girl who wore the latest Jordans as soon as they were released and the "gold girl," always adorned with multiple necklaces and rings on nearly every finger.

Despite everything, he never deprived me of anything. He ensured I had a supportive circle by encouraging interactions with family and friends. Though I missed my mom dearly—an irreplaceable part of my life—he went above and beyond to keep me happy and loved.

Looking back, I now realize the sacrifices he made. It could not have been easy to juggle the demands of work, parenting, and his own healing. Yet, through his perseverance and faith, he became my rock. In many ways, his love and dedication were a reflection of the strength my mother had prayed for before I was even born.

He earns an award for being the *Best Dad Ever*. This award is based on a reflection of his unwavering love, dedication and sacrifice in raising me. He did not just provide for my physical needs. He was a constant source of emotional support, guidance and encouragement. As a single father, he faced challenges that many might consider insurmountable, but he never let those obstacles define him. Instead, he found strength in God and in his love for me and his desire to see me thrive.

This award symbolizes more than just a recognition. It represents his resilience, determination and faith in God's ability to equip him to raise me on his own. Through every struggle, he was my protector, my provider, and my teacher. His example of selflessness and commitment continues to inspire me as I look back on all the sacrifices he made to ensure I had everything I needed to succeed in life.

As I reflect on this, I realize that the true essence of being the *Best Dad Ever* goes beyond accolades. It is in the quiet, everyday moments where love and devotion shine the brightest. My dad's unwavering commitment to me, despite the difficulties of being a single father, shaped who I am today, and I am forever grateful for the legacy he created in my life.

I went from grief to gratitude, learning to truly appreciate having my dad in my life and all the sacrifices he made for me. What once felt like a source of pain became a deep well of thankfulness as I recognized his unwavering love, strength and dedication. His presence, guidance and everything he did for me became the foundation of my gratitude. Over time, I shifted from focusing on what I lacked to celebrating the incredible blessings he gave me every day. I am still grateful to have him in my life.

Though we were set back by my mother's loss, God's plan for our lives did not end there. Her absence became a part of our story— a painful chapter, yes, but one that shaped us into who we were meant to become. And even in that sorrow, God was with us, guiding us through the darkness into His light.

Looking back, I see God's hand in every moment. Though we lost my mother, God filled the gaps in ways only He could. He healed the brokenness, carried us through the hardest days, and turned our mourning into purpose. My mother's legacy and my father's unwavering love are reminders that even in loss, God's grace is sufficient. He turns pain into testimony and loss into a deeper understanding of His faithfulness.

Grief is a profound emotional experience that can deeply affect both the **physical** and **spiritual** aspects of a person's life. It occurs when we experience loss, whether it be the death of a loved one, the end of a relationship, or the loss of a dream or expectation. The effects of grief are not just emotional. They also manifest in our bodies and spirits.

**Physical Grief**

Grief impacts the **body** in various ways. The stress and emotional turmoil from loss can create a range of physical symptoms, as the body and mind are closely connected. Some common physical effects of grief include:

1. **Fatigue and Exhaustion**: The emotional toll of grief often leaves a person feeling drained and fatigued. It's as if the weight of the sadness takes a toll on your energy, making it difficult to function normally.
2. **Appetite Changes**: Grieving individuals may experience a loss of appetite or, conversely, an increase in eating as a way to cope with emotions. These changes in eating habits can affect a person's health and well-being.
3. **Sleep Disturbances**: Grief can cause sleep problems, such as insomnia or excessive sleeping. Nighttime often brings

heightened emotions or intrusive thoughts, making it harder to rest and recover.

4. **Physical Pain**: Some people experience physical pain such as headaches, stomachaches, or muscle tension during grief. These pains can often be traced back to the emotional stress that is being carried in the body.

5. **Weakened Immune System**: The stress of grief can lower the body's ability to fight illness, leading to an increased susceptibility to colds, infections, or other health issues.

## Spiritual Grief

On a **spiritual** level, grief can shake a person's faith and relationship with God or their understanding of life's meaning. The pain of loss often raises deep existential questions, and it can cause spiritual turmoil. Here are a few ways grief can impact the spirit:

1. **Loss of Faith or Doubt**: Many people experience doubt in their faith during periods of grief. They may question why the loss occurred, why God allowed it, or why they must go through such suffering. This can lead to a feeling of spiritual emptiness or even a crisis of faith.

2. **Feelings of Abandonment**: In the midst of grief, some individuals may feel disconnected from God, as if they are alone in their pain. These feelings can be intense, and they may lead someone to question their worth or whether God still cares for them.

3. **Desire for Healing and Restoration**: Grief can create a deep longing for restoration or a desire for a sense of peace and comfort. People may turn to prayer, Scripture or meditation to seek solace and healing, looking for spiritual renewal in the face of sorrow.

4. **Spiritual Transformation**: While grief can lead to spiritual struggles, it can also lead to growth and transformation. In

some cases, grief prompts individuals to draw closer to God, seeking comfort and understanding in their faith. This spiritual journey may lead to a deeper connection with God, greater compassion for others, and a renewed sense of purpose.

5. **Forgiveness and Release**: Sometimes, grief brings up the need for forgiveness—whether it is forgiving others or even forgiving ourselves. Spiritually, the process of forgiving and releasing negative emotions can bring healing to the heart and soul.

Grief is a complex journey that affects the whole person—body, mind and spirit—but it is also a path that can lead to healing, growth, and renewed strength. Through it, many discover deeper layers of resilience and faith, finding hope and purpose in the midst of sorrow.

## Mindset Shift

Losing a loved one is undoubtedly one of life's most painful experiences. The grief and sorrow can be overwhelming, and it is easy to find ourselves consumed by what we have lost. We mourn the moments that will never come, the conversations that will never happen, and the future that will never unfold with that person by our side. But in the midst of the pain, there is an important shift in perspective that can bring healing - focusing not on what you have lost, but on what you have gained.

When we lose someone dear, we often forget the ways in which they have enriched our lives. The lessons they taught us, the memories we shared, and the love they gave us become treasures that remain, even after they are gone. Their impact on our lives is a part of us, shaping who we are and who we become. We gain a deeper understanding of love, compassion, and the value of time.

We gain a perspective that allows us to cherish the people around us even more, appreciating each moment as precious and fleeting.

Additionally, the loss can bring about a strengthening of our faith and resilience. In the face of sorrow, we often find new depths of courage, endurance, and trust in God. We may discover that we are capable of handling far more than we ever thought possible, relying on the strength God provides. We are carried through it with grace, comfort, and the assurance that we are not alone.

While the grief is real, focusing on what you have gained can shift your mindset. You begin to see that the love shared was never in vain, that the relationship shaped you into the person you are today. You may also gain a renewed sense of purpose, understanding that life is fleeting, and it is important to live it fully. Through loss, we may find that we gain wisdom, a deeper connection to God, and a greater appreciation for the people who remain.

In your time of sorrow, take a moment to reflect on the love, the lessons, and the strength you have gained. While you may never fully understand why the loss occurred, what you gained in the relationship can never be taken away.

**Overcoming the Loss of a Loved One in Jesus**

The loss of a loved one is one of life's most profound and painful experiences. It can leave us feeling broken, empty and overwhelmed by grief. However, as followers of Jesus, we have access to a unique source of comfort and hope. God meets us in our pain, walks with us through the valley of sorrow, and offers us the promise of eternal life—a promise that transforms our grief into a journey of healing and faith.

1. Acknowledge Your Grief

Grief is a natural response to loss. Jesus Himself experienced sorrow when His friend Lazarus died, and He wept alongside those who mourned (John 11:35). Allow yourself to feel the pain of your loss and express your emotions openly to God. Suppressing grief can prolong healing, but bringing your pain to Jesus opens the door for His comfort.

Scripture for Reflection: *"Blessed are they that mourn: for they shall be comforted."* (Matthew 5:4)

2. Seek God's Presence

In moments of deep sorrow, draw near to God. His presence brings peace that surpasses understanding, even in the midst of heartache. Spend time in prayer, worship and meditation on His Word. When words fail, allow the Holy Spirit to intercede for you with groans too deep for words (Romans 8:26).

Scripture for Reflection: *"The LORD is nigh unto them that are of a broken heart; and saveth such as be of a contrite spirit."* (Psalm 34:18)

3. Hold on to the Hope of Eternity

One of the greatest comforts for believers is the promise of eternal life. Through Jesus, death is not the end. For those who have accepted Christ, it is a transition to eternal fellowship with Him. While the pain of separation is real, the hope of being reunited in heaven offers profound comfort.

Scripture for Reflection: *"And God shall wipe away all tears from their eyes; and there shall be no more death, neither sorrow, nor crying, neither shall there be any more pain: for the former things are passed away."* (Revelation 21:4)

4. Lean on Community

Grief can feel isolating, but God has given us the gift of community. Surround yourself with people who will support and encourage you. Share your feelings with trusted friends, family, or a church group. Let others pray for you and walk alongside you in this season of sorrow.

Scripture for Reflection: *"Bear ye one another's burdens, and so fulfil the law of Christ."* (Galatians 6:2 KJV)

5. Find Purpose in the Pain

While we may never fully understand why we lose loved ones, God can use our pain for a greater purpose. Sharing your testimony of healing and hope can encourage others who are grieving. Your journey can be a reminder that God brings beauty from ashes and joy from mourning.

Scripture for Reflection: *"And we know that all things work together for good to them that love God, to them who are the called according to his purpose."* (Romans 8:28 KJV)

6. Trust God's Timing for Healing

Healing from grief is not linear and cannot be rushed. Trust God's timing as He works in your heart. Allow yourself to experience moments of joy without guilt and remember that healing does not mean forgetting. It means moving forward with the memories and love you shared.

Scripture for Reflection: *"To every thing there is a season, and a time to every purpose under the heaven: a time to be born, and a time to die; a time to plant, and a time to pluck up that which is planted; a time to kill, and a time to heal; a time to break down, and a time to build up; a time to weep, and a time to laugh; a time to mourn, and a time to dance."* (Ecclesiastes 3:1-4)

7. Rely on God's Strength

When the weight of grief feels unbearable, lean on God's strength. He is your refuge and source of endurance. In your weakness, His power is made perfect (2 Corinthians 12:9). Trust Him to carry you through, one day at a time.

Scripture for Reflection: *"God is our refuge and strength, a very present help in trouble."* (Psalm 46:1)

**Spirit of Grief**

Grief is a natural and necessary process when we experience the loss of a loved one. It is a time of mourning, reflection and healing. However, during this vulnerable season, we must remain spiritually vigilant, as the enemy often seeks to exploit our pain and turn it into an opportunity for destruction.

Demonic influence in grief can manifest in subtle yet damaging ways. The enemy whispers lies, such as blaming God for the loss, fostering bitterness, or convincing us we will never recover. These thoughts can lead to isolation, despair, and even a turning away from faith. The devil preys on our weakest moments, seeking to deepen our sorrow and steal our hope.

Another tactic is planting seeds of guilt or condemnation. Thoughts like, *"I should have done more"* or *"It's my fault they're gone"* can weigh heavily on our hearts. These are not from God but are strategies designed to trap us in a cycle of self-blame and spiritual paralysis.

The enemy also tries to open doors to unhealthy coping mechanisms. In grief, people may turn to addiction, anger, or unhealthy relationships as a means of escape. What starts as a search for comfort can lead to spiritual bondage, leaving the person further broken and disconnected from God.

But there is hope and victory through Christ. Recognizing these attacks is the first step to overcoming them. God has given us His Word, His Spirit, and the power of prayer to combat the enemy's schemes. When feelings of despair, guilt or bitterness arise, we must take those thoughts captive and replace them with God's truth. Scriptures like Psalm 34:18 remind us that *"The LORD is nigh unto them that are of a broken heart; and saveth such as be of a contrite spirit."*

Prayer is a powerful weapon. Invite God into your grief, asking Him to heal your heart and guard your mind against the lies of the enemy. Surround yourself with godly counsel and community who can support you in prayer and remind you of God's promises. Worship, even in your pain, invites God's presence and pushes back the darkness.

Ultimately, grief is not the enemy—Satan is. God can use your mourning to draw you closer to Him, to deepen your faith, and to bring beauty from ashes. The enemy may try to exploit your grief, but he cannot defeat you when you remain rooted in God's love and truth. Victory is yours, even in the valley of sorrow.

Sometimes, when experiencing grief, a person can find themselves struggling with emotions that seem overwhelming and persistent, going beyond the natural process of mourning. In these cases, a spirit of grief can enter in, and it can manifest in ways that hinder emotional and spiritual healing. While grief is a natural and necessary response to loss, a spirit of grief is a spiritual attack that can cause an individual to remain stuck in prolonged sorrow, despair and hopelessness, making it difficult to heal or move forward.

The spirit of grief is a spiritual force that can latch onto a person's emotions, preventing them from finding peace or joy. It can keep them trapped in an unending cycle of mourning, sadness, and even depression. Unlike natural grief, which has an eventual healing process, the spirit of grief can distort one's perception of reality and make it harder to experience any form of relief. It can also lead to an overwhelming sense of hopelessness or helplessness, making the person feel as though they will never heal from their loss.

**Signs of the Spirit of Grief**

Here are a few signs that a person may be dealing with the spirit of grief:

1. **Prolonged Sorrow**: While grief is normal after a loss, a spirit of grief can cause sorrow that persists far beyond what is typical. This can be marked by an inability to experience joy, even when circumstances change or when other areas of life improve.
2. **Isolation**: Individuals under the influence of the spirit of grief may withdraw from others, avoiding social interactions, and may feel disconnected or abandoned. This isolation can deepen the sorrow, preventing healing.
3. **Physical Manifestations**: The spirit of grief can manifest in physical ways, such as chronic fatigue, difficulty sleeping, loss of appetite, or constant physical pain. These symptoms may persist even when there is no underlying medical cause, exacerbating the emotional pain.
4. **Overwhelming Despair**: The spirit of grief often brings a deep sense of hopelessness and helplessness, convincing the individual that healing is impossible. This despair can lead to negative thought patterns and even suicidal ideation.
5. **Unforgiveness or Bitterness**: Sometimes, the spirit of grief can bring unresolved anger or bitterness, either toward the

situation or toward people who may have been involved in the loss. This can prevent true healing, as unforgiveness is often a barrier to emotional and spiritual peace.

When a spirit of grief is at work, it is important to recognize that this is not something that can always be healed through time alone or by simply "waiting it out." In such cases, seeking deliverance from someone who specializes in spiritual matters—like a pastor, counselor, or deliverance minister—can help break the stronghold of the spirit of grief. Deliverance is the process of being set free from spiritual oppression or strongholds that hinder a person's well-being.

A deliverance minister will typically use prayer, spiritual authority, and specific biblical teachings to help the individual break free from the spirit of grief. While natural grief is part of the healing process, a spirit of grief can keep someone in a prolonged state of sadness and despair. It can rob them of their joy, keep them from finding peace, and prevent them from fully healing. Deliverance from the spirit of grief allows an individual to break free from the emotional and spiritual oppression, enabling them to heal, restore their joy, and walk in the fullness of God's peace.

In these moments, it is important to remember that deliverance is not a sign of weakness, but rather an act of faith in God's ability to heal, restore, and set us free. If you discern you are dealing with a spirit of grief, seeking deliverance from someone who is equipped to help is a powerful step toward emotional and spiritual healing. Through prayer, support and deliverance, you can experience freedom from grief's stronghold and move into a season of restoration, hope and healing.

**Message of Hope**

Losing someone you love is one of the hardest experiences to endure. The pain can feel overwhelming, and the emptiness they leave behind is difficult to put into words. But even in the midst of your grief, there is hope.

You are not alone. God sees your tears, hears your prayers, and feels your heartache. He is near to the brokenhearted and promises to carry you through this season of loss. Lean on Him, for His love is constant and unchanging, even when life feels uncertain.

Know that your loved one's life had purpose and meaning, and their legacy lives on through the impact they made. Remember the joy they brought, the lessons they taught, and the love they shared. Hold onto those memories as a source of comfort and strength.

The promise of eternity reminds us that this goodbye is not forever. For those in Christ, there is the hope of reunion in heaven, where there will be no more tears, no more pain, and no more death. Until that day comes, trust that God is walking with you, guiding you, and restoring you.

Take heart. You are stronger than you feel right now, and brighter days are ahead. Your loved one may be gone, but their love remains forever in your heart. And God's love will never let you go.

**Declaration**

In the name of Jesus, I declare that I am healed from the pain of losing my loved one. Though their absence left a void, God has filled that space with His peace, comfort, and unfailing love. I acknowledge the grief, but I refuse to let it define me or hold me captive. I declare that God has turned my mourning into dancing and my sorrow into joy. He has strengthened me in my weakness and given me beauty for ashes. My heart is no longer weighed down by despair because I trust in the LORD, who is close to the brokenhearted and saves those who are crushed in spirit. I choose to celebrate the life of my loved one, cherishing the memories and the impact they had on me. I accept that their purpose on this earth was fulfilled and that God, in His sovereignty, has a plan greater than I can see. I declare that the love of God surrounds me daily, bringing comfort and hope for the future. I walk forward in faith, knowing that God restores and renews. I release all bitterness, regret, and unanswered questions, and I embrace the healing power of Christ, who makes all things new. In Jesus' name, I am whole, restored and free. Amen.

# Testimony #3:
# Rebellion to Redemption

**2 Corinthians 5:17**
*"Therefore if any man be in Christ, he is a new creature: old things are passed away; behold, all things are become new."*

My testimony begins in Hartford, Connecticut, where I grew up surrounded by influences that led me down a path of rebellion. As a teenager, I found myself in a difficult environment, where many of my friends were involved in gangs. The lure of belonging, power and protection that came with gang life seemed tempting, especially in a place where survival often meant aligning with the wrong crowd. At the time, I did not fully understand the danger I was courting, nor did I realize the deep consequences that could have come from those connections.

Along with my gang association, I was also drawn to the club scene. I almost became fully involved in it, believing the excitement and the temporary sense of freedom would give me the escape I was craving. Music, too, was a major influence. I listened to songs that glorified rebellion, partying, and reckless behavior. The lyrics seemed to speak to me, fueling a desire to escape reality, ignore authority, and live for the moment.

I often disregarded my dad's instructions and chose to do things my own way. We argued frequently, and I had major tantrums that sometimes led to breaking things. I surrounded myself with friends who were not the best influence, and I consistently did the opposite of what my dad asked of me.

During those years, I also began to hide my drinking from my dad. Alcohol became a way to numb the pain and frustration I was feeling inside. I would sneak around, trying to drink in secret, hoping my actions would not be discovered. I would go out late with my friends, often returning home after curfew, feeling like I was living life on my terms. I was searching for freedom but did not realize I was walking deeper into bondage.

One of the defining moments during this time was when I got into a fight. It was not something I planned or wanted, but the anger and pressure around me led to a physical confrontation. I remember the tension, the rising emotions, and the sense that I might get pulled into something much darker. But in that moment, and many others like it, God's protection was evident. Every time I was about to get into a fight or a situation that could have led to further harm, the person I was meant to clash with never showed up. It was as though the enemy's plans were constantly thwarted. I never fully realized it at the time, but I can see now that God was watching over me, even when I was heading down the wrong path.

In those years, I would often say, *"I can't wait until I turn 18 and get out of my dad's house."* I believed that once I turned 18, I would be free. Free from the rules, free from restrictions, and free to live life how I wanted. I thought that freedom would come through independence and breaking away from the structure my father had provided. What I did not understand was that the kind of freedom I was seeking was not the kind I would find by leaving home or following the ways of the world. It was a freedom that could only be found in Christ—a freedom from the chains of sin, rebellion and destruction.

I grew up with a foundation of faith, but I began to stray from it as I got older. The world around me seemed more appealing—its distractions and promises of fulfillment. I thought I knew better than anyone else, including God. I indulged in things that pulled me farther away from the peace I once knew. I was stubborn, prideful and distant from the very source of my life.

In the midst of my rebellion, God had a different plan for me. I did not know it at the time, but He was working behind the scenes, gently but persistently calling me back. And then came a moment that would change everything—a moment I never could have predicted.

In hindsight, I can see all of the moments where I almost got caught up in fights or dangerous situations were divine interventions. God's protection was there even when I was not seeking it, sparing me from consequences that could have changed the course of my life. I realize now that my desire for freedom was misguided. I was searching for something I did not fully understand, and I needed to be broken free from the things that kept me bound.

Remember when I used to say, *"I can't wait until I turn 18 to leave my dad's house and be free?"* Well, that is exactly what happened—but not in the way I expected. The freedom I thought I would gain was not the freedom I truly needed. Instead of finding independence on my own terms, God led me to upstate New York, where my journey took a completely different turn.

It was there, under the guidance of my uncle—who is also my apostle—where I accepted Jesus Christ as my LORD and Savior. I thought I was stepping into one kind of freedom, but God had a greater plan. The true freedom I longed for did not come from leaving home or doing things my way. It came through surrendering my life to Christ.

Upon my arrival in upstate New York, I found myself living with my uncle, a man who was not only a pastor but also a prophet. He and his wife became my spiritual parents. Their home was not just a refuge from the chaos of my life, but a sanctuary where God's love and wisdom were poured into me daily. My uncle's guidance, his prophetic insight, and his deep understanding of God's word challenged me to grow in ways I never anticipated. And my aunt, with her nurturing heart and unwavering faith, provided the love and support I so desperately needed.

Living with them was not always easy. There were challenges, not just from the adjustments of living in a new place, but also from my own family. Many of my relatives did not understand why I chose to be under my uncle's ministry. They did not see the significance of the spiritual nurturing that was happening in my life. Some questioned my decision, others criticized it, but deep down, I knew it was part of God's plan for me.

It was not just about finding a place to stay. It was about finding a place to grow—spiritually, emotionally and mentally. I understood I needed to be under a ministry that could equip me to become the disciple God was calling me to be. My uncle and aunt's home became that ministry. They did not just provide a roof over my head—they pushed me to be the best disciple I could be. They encouraged me to delve deeper into God's Word, to strengthen my prayer life, and to embrace the call that God had placed on my life. Their ministry was not just about teaching—it was about equipping me for the work God had ahead of me.

There were times when I felt torn between the familiar voices of family members who did not understand my new path and the quiet voice of God, calling me to remain focused on His plan for my life. It would have been easier to give in to the pressure, to let the doubts and criticisms sway me, but God gave me the strength to stay focused. I had to trust that His plan was greater than the opinions of others. I had to believe that being under the ministry of my uncle and aunt was where I needed to be to grow into the person God intended me to be.

It was not always comfortable. There were moments when I felt misunderstood and when the weight of family disapproval seemed heavy. But those were the moments that tested my faith, moments that refined my character, and moments that strengthened my resolve to follow God's leading. Through it all, my uncle and aunt remained unwavering in their support, always guiding me back to the Word of God, reminding me of my purpose, and pushing me to be the best version of myself in Christ.

Looking back, I realize my time living with my uncle and aunt was not just a season of physical relocation—it was a season of spiritual renewal and growth. It was a time of laying down my own desires and fully surrendering to God's will. God used my uncle and aunt to nurture me, shape me, and equip me for the calling He had placed on my life. And even though it was hard at times, I know it was all part of God's perfect plan to bring me closer to Him and to mold me into the disciple I am today.

Though the process was not instant, I began to walk in a freedom far greater than anything I had imagined. It was a journey of transformation, healing, and learning to live in the fullness of God's purpose for my life. Looking back, I see God was not taking me away from freedom—He was leading me into it.

It was in this new place, surrounded by the beauty of nature and the quiet stillness of upstate New York, that I encountered a deep spiritual awakening. I began to understand the gravity of God's grace in a way I never had before. The rebellious spirit that had once defined me began to break down, piece by piece, as I recognized I could never truly escape the love of God.

God's mercy met me where I was—broken, lost, and full of regret. But His grace lifted me, gave me purpose, and turned my life in a new direction. I found freedom not in rebellion, but in surrender. Surrender to the One who had always loved me, even when I rejected Him. He not only saved me from my past, but He also gave me a hope for my future that I had never known before.

My move to upstate New York was not just a physical relocation—it was a spiritual journey. A journey of redemption, healing and renewal. God used that time to speak to me, to restore my soul, and to remind me that no matter how far I had wandered, I was never too far from His grace.

This chapter of my life is a testimony to the power of God's love and redemption. Even in our rebellion, God is faithful. He pursues us, He saves us, and He brings us back to where we belong. And for that, I will forever be grateful. He led me to the right place, surrounded me with the right people, and placed me under the right ministry at just the right time. Through their nurturing, guidance, and prayers, I grew in ways I never could have on my own. I am forever grateful for the spiritual foundation that was laid in those years—foundations that continue to support me as I walk out God's purpose for my life. When I look back on my life, I can clearly see how God orchestrated every step, even when I did not understand the path He was leading me down.

My testimony is a reminder that even in our darkest moments, God is still at work, protecting and guiding us. Despite the rebellion, the toxic influences, and the risky decisions, God was faithful to keep me, and I now see how His protection and love were at work in my life, even when I was not fully aware of it. Today, I am grateful for His mercy, for His deliverance, and for the true freedom that comes in surrendering to His will. True freedom came when I surrendered my life to God and allowed Him to transform me. He showed me that the path to real freedom is found in obedience to Him, not in rebellion against the world.

**The Origination of Rebellion**

Rebellion is one of Satan's most powerful weapons against God's people. It was rebellion that led to his own downfall, and it is the same tactic he uses to deceive and destroy others.

Satan, originally known as Lucifer, was once a high-ranking angel in heaven. He was full of wisdom, beauty, and held a place of honor among God's creation. However, pride entered his heart, and he desired to exalt himself above God. Isaiah 14:12-15 describes his rebellion: *"How art thou fallen from heaven, O Lucifer, son of the morning! how art thou cut down to the ground, which didst weaken the nations! For thou hast said in thine heart, I will ascend into heaven, I will exalt my throne above the stars of God: I will sit also upon the mount of the congregation, in the sides of the north: I will ascend above the heights of the clouds; I will be like the most High. Yet thou shalt be brought down to hell, to the sides of the pit."*

Satan's rebellion was rooted in **pride, self-exaltation, and disobedience**. Instead of submitting to God's authority, he sought to overthrow it. As a result, he was cast out of heaven, stripped of his position, and became the adversary of God and His people.

Just as Satan fell through rebellion, he uses the same strategy to lead people away from God. Rebellion against parents, spiritual leaders, or God's commands opens doors for deception and destruction. The enemy whispers lies that make disobedience seem like freedom, but in reality, it is a trap that leads to bondage.

1 Samuel 15:23 warns, *"For rebellion is as the sin of witchcraft, and stubbornness is as iniquity and idolatry. Because thou hast rejected the word of the LORD, he hath also rejected thee from being king."* This verse reveals that rebellion is not just a minor act of disobedience—it is a serious spiritual issue that aligns a person with darkness rather than with God.

Satan's goal is to make people reject God's order, His truth, and His authority, just as he did. But when we recognize rebellion for what it is—a tool of the enemy—we can resist it and walk in the freedom that comes through submission to God's will. True freedom is not found in rebellion, but in obedience to the One who created us.

**An Encouragement to the Rebellious Heart**

If you are reading this and find yourself in a place of rebellion, I want to speak directly to your heart. I know the road of rebellion can feel like the only road worth walking—like you are in control, making your own decisions, and living life on your terms. But deep down, there is often a feeling of emptiness, a longing for something more, something real, something that can only be found in the love and grace of God.

I want you to know that no matter how far you have wandered, God's love is always there, waiting for you. You may feel like you do not want to hear the word of God, or like it is too late for you to turn around. But I assure you, it is never too late. No matter how many times you have turned your back, God is still reaching out to you with open arms.

The Bible says, *"For the Son of Man came to seek and to save the lost"* (Luke 19:10). That includes you. God sees you in your rebellion, in your hurt, and in your struggle. He is not angry with you—He is not waiting to punish you. He is patiently waiting for you to return to Him, because He loves you with an unshakable, unconditional love that never fades.

I know it might be hard to believe right now, but God's plan for your life is better than anything you can imagine. The world promises satisfaction, but it leaves you wanting more. The things that seem fulfilling are only temporary, but God offers lasting peace, joy and purpose that cannot be shaken.

If you are struggling to accept His love, I encourage you to take one small step—just open your heart and allow Him to speak to you. Even if you do not want to hear it, even if you are angry or confused, God is still reaching out. The word of God is living and powerful, and when you let it in, it has the power to heal, restore and transform.

You do not have to walk this path of rebellion alone. There are people who love you, who are praying for you, and who will stand beside you as you find your way back to the LORD. I encourage you to listen to your parents and those in authority who genuinely have your best interest at heart. Their guidance comes from wisdom and experience, and embracing it can help you avoid unnecessary struggles and walk in the right path. I encourage you to reach out, to ask questions, and to open your heart to the possibility of a life lived in surrender to God's will.

It will not be easy, and the road may be challenging, but I promise you that it will be worth it. God's love is greater than anything you have experienced, and His plans for your life are far beyond what you can comprehend. Allow Him to lead you, to guide you, and to show you the peace and purpose that come from truly surrendering to Him.

You are not too far gone, and it is never too late to turn back to the One who created you. Let His love find you, heal you, and set you free.

1. **Acknowledge Your Need for Change**
   Before overcoming rebellion, it is essential to recognize the need for transformation. Scripture encourages us to examine our hearts:
   - *"Search me, O God, and know my heart: try me, and know my thoughts."* (Psalm 139:23)
   - *"If we confess our sins, he is faithful and just to forgive us our sins, and to cleanse us from all unrighteousness."* (1 John 1:9)

2. **Repent and Seek Forgiveness**

   Repentance is the first step in returning to God. It involves turning away from rebellion and turning toward Him.

   - *"Repent, then, and turn to God, so that your sins may be wiped out, that times of refreshing may come from the Lord."* (Acts 3:19)
   - *"The Lord is close to the brokenhearted and saves those who are crushed in spirit."* (Psalm 34:18)

3. **Surrender Your Will to God**

   Rebellion often arises from our desire to control. Surrendering to God's will allows His power to transform us.

   - *"Not my will, but yours be done."* (Luke 22:42)
   - *"Trust in the Lord with all your heart and lean not on your own understanding; in all your ways submit to him, and he will make your paths straight."* (Proverbs 3:5-6 NIV)

4. **Renew Your Mind with God's Word**

   Align your thoughts with God's truth. Meditate on Scripture to change your mindset and overcome rebellion.

   - *"Do not conform to the pattern of this world, but be transformed by the renewing of your mind."* (Romans 12:2 NIV)
   - *"Your word is a lamp for my feet, a light on my path."* (Psalm 119:105 NIV)

5. **Obey God's Commands**

   Obedience to God is the key to overcoming rebellion. When you submit to God's authority, you experience freedom and peace.

   - *"If you love me, keep my commands."* (John 14:15 NIV)

- o *"But be doers of the word, and not hearers only, deceiving yourselves."* (James 1:22 NKJV)

6. **Embrace Humility and Repentance**

   Rebellion often comes from pride. Humble yourself before God and acknowledge His sovereignty.

   - o *"Humble yourselves, therefore, under God's mighty hand, that he may lift you up in due time."* (1 Peter 5:6)
   - o *"God opposes the proud but shows favor to the humble."* (James 4:6)

7. **Find Strength in God's Grace**

   God's grace is sufficient for us, even in our weakness. Lean on His grace as you overcome rebellion.

   - o *"But he said to me, 'My grace is sufficient for you, for my power is made perfect in weakness.' Therefore I will boast all the more gladly of my weaknesses, so that the power of Christ may rest upon me."* (2 Corinthians 12:9)
   - o *"The Lord will fight for you; you need only to be still."* (Exodus 14:14)

8. **Seek Godly Counsel and Fellowship**

   Surround yourself with people who will help you stay on track, provide wisdom, and encourage obedience.

   - o *"Plans fail for lack of counsel, but with many advisers they succeed."* (Proverbs 15:22)
   - o *"As iron sharpens iron, so one person sharpens another."* (Proverbs 27:17)

9. **Walk in the Freedom of Obedience**

   As you turn away from rebellion, embrace the freedom found in living according to God's Word.

   - o *"So if the Son sets you free, you will be free indeed."* (John 8:36)
   - o *"Where the Spirit of the Lord is, there is freedom."* (2 Corinthians 3:17)

10. **Keep Persevering in Faith**

   The journey from rebellion to redemption takes time, but God's faithfulness will sustain you.

   - *"Let us not become weary in doing good, for at the proper time we will reap a harvest if we do not give up."* (Galatians 6:9)
   - *"I can do all things through him who gives me strength."* (Philippians 4:13)

## Spirit of Rebellion

Rebellion is a spiritual force that opposes God's authority, His Word, and His established order. Rooted in pride, disobedience, and rejection of divine authority, the demonic spirit of rebellion is a powerful tool the enemy uses to sow discord, disrupt relationships, and distance individuals from God's will. It works subtly and deceptively, often masquerading as independence or self-empowerment, but its true nature is to lead people away from obedience to God.

The spirit of rebellion is a dangerous and deceptive force that leads people away from God's will, causing them to reject His authority and guidance. Rebellion is not just an act of disobedience; it is a spiritual stronghold that can take root in a person's heart, influencing their thoughts, attitudes and actions.

Rebellion often begins subtly—through pride, stubbornness, or a desire for independence outside of God's order. The enemy whispers lies, making disobedience seem like freedom. However, true freedom comes from submission to God, not from rejecting Him. When rebellion becomes stubborn and deeply rooted, it can manifest in different ways, such as: refusal to submit to authority (parents, pastors, teachers, or even God), constant resistance to correction or instruction, a hardened heart that rejects conviction, justifying sinful behavior, rejecting biblical truth, and destructive behavior patterns that keep a person bound.

If rebellion becomes stubborn and persistent, it may require deliverance—a spiritual breakthrough where the stronghold is broken through prayer, fasting, and seeking someone anointed for deliverance ministry. Sometimes, people try to change on their own but struggle because the spirit of rebellion has taken deep root in their life.

**Message of Hope**

To those who feel lost, distant or rebellious, know that there is always hope, no matter where you find yourself. Even in moments when you stray from the path, remember God's love is unshakeable and His grace is ever-present. No matter how far you wander, His arms are open, waiting for you to return.

Rebellion may feel like a form of freedom, but true peace and purpose are found in aligning with God's will. His plans for you are greater than anything you could imagine, and His forgiveness is abundant. It's never too late to turn back, to seek His guidance, and to find healing.

You are deeply loved, valued, and never beyond redemption. God's promises stand firm, and His mercy is new every morning. You do not have to walk this road alone. He is with you, guiding you toward restoration. Keep pressing forward, for hope is alive, and a new beginning is always possible.

**Declaration**

I declare today that I am no longer bound by rebellion or the weight of my past. I choose to turn away from my old ways and embrace the love and grace that is offered to me. I am no longer defined by my mistakes, my struggles, or my brokenness. I am choosing redemption. I acknowledge that I have strayed, but I believe God's arms are wide open, ready to receive me. I claim His forgiveness, His healing, and His transforming power over my life. I declare I will no longer walk in the darkness of my rebellion, but I will walk in the light of His truth. I am set free. I am redeemed. I am restored. The old is gone, and the new has come. I choose to trust in God's plans for my life, knowing they are filled with hope, purpose and peace. I am no longer a slave to sin, but a child of God, redeemed and forgiven. In this moment, I declare my journey of redemption begins. I will follow His lead, for He is faithful to complete the good work He has started in me. My past does not define me. His grace does. I am redeemed!

# Testimony #4
# The Power of the Holy Spirit

**Acts 2:4 KJV**
*"And they were all filled with the Holy Ghost, and began to speak with other tongues, as the Spirit gave them utterance."*

In 2011, a new chapter began in my life—one I never could have imagined. That year marked not only my salvation but the beginning of my journey into the deeper things of God. It was a year that would change my life forever, and it all started with hearing about the Holy Spirit. I had heard people speak in tongues, and honestly, I thought it was strange. At the time, it was something I could not quite understand. It seemed foreign to me, and I could not grasp how or why people would express their faith in that way.

But as I spent more time in church, learning, growing, and seeking a closer relationship with God, I began to feel a hunger rising within me—a deep desire to experience the Holy Spirit in the same way I had witnessed others do. I wanted to know the fullness of what it meant to be filled with the Spirit. I wanted that same power and presence to transform my life. And so, I began to pray earnestly, asking God to fill me with His Holy Spirit.

One day when three of us gathered together, and my uncle—who had become a spiritual mentor—prayed over us. We were all believing for the baptism of the Holy Spirit, for that powerful, life-changing encounter. My uncle prayed fervently, and after a moment of prayer, one of us was filled with the Holy Spirit—but it was not me. In that moment, I felt a deep discouragement wash over me. I had been so hungry for this experience, and yet I had not received it. The enemy tried to make me question if I was worthy, if I had done something wrong, or if it was just never meant to happen for me.

But in that moment of discouragement, God spoke to my heart. He reminded me that it was not His time yet, and that I needed to keep having faith. He assured me that His timing was perfect, and that I needed to trust Him as I continued to seek and believe. So, I chose not to give up, even though my heart felt heavy. I chose to trust that the Holy Spirit would come in His time.

Then one day, while I was in church, it happened suddenly. I can still remember the moment clearly. It was not something I had planned or expected, but as I sat there in the pew, I felt an overwhelming sense of God's presence. Without warning, I was filled with the Holy Spirit. The power, the fire, the love—it overwhelmed me in a way I had never experienced before. It was as though a floodgate had opened, and all the fears, doubts, and discouragements that had held me back were washed away.

Getting filled with the Holy Spirit radically changed my life. It transformed my walk with God. The boldness I had prayed for came with that baptism of fire. Before that moment, I was terrified of public speaking, held back by the fear of being judged or making a mistake. But once I received the Holy Spirit, something shifted. God gave me a new boldness, a courage I did not know I had, to preach His Word. I began to speak with authority and conviction, sharing the Gospel with others in a way that was once unimaginable for me.

The enemy still tries to bring fear, trying to remind me of my past insecurities or doubt my ability. But I overcame it, not by my own strength, but by stepping out in faith and doing what God has called me to do. Every time I face that fear, I know the Holy Spirit is with me, empowering me to overcome and fulfill the call on my life.

When the Holy Spirit baptizes you with fire, it does not just change your moment—it changes your entire walk with God. It brings a deep sense of purpose, power and passion for His kingdom. It equips you to do what you could not do on your own and gives you the boldness to step into the plans God has prepared for you. And it is not a one-time experience—it is a continual journey of growing in His power and presence.

My life will never be the same because of the Holy Spirit. That encounter changed everything—from my faith to my ministry to the way I walk with God every single day. And if you are hungry for more of God, I encourage you to seek the Holy Spirit. He is ready to fill you, empower you, and transform you into the person God has called you to be. Keep pressing, keep believing, and in God's perfect timing, He will fill you with the fire that will change your life forever.

**The Power of the Holy Spirit**

The Holy Spirit is the third person of the Trinity—fully God, all-powerful, and ever-present. He is not just a force or an influence but a divine person who empowers, leads and transforms the lives of believers. Jesus emphasized the importance of the Holy Spirit when He told His disciples, *"But ye shall receive power, after that the Holy Ghost is come upon you: and ye shall be witnesses unto me both in Jerusalem, and in all Judaea, and in Samaria, and unto the uttermost part of the earth."* (Acts 1:8)

The Holy Spirit gives **power** to:

- **Break strongholds** – The anointing of the Holy Spirit destroys yokes of bondage (Isaiah 10:27).
- **Equip believers for ministry** – He imparts spiritual gifts for the edification of the church (1 Corinthians 12:7-11).

- **Guide into all truth** – He reveals the mysteries of God and gives wisdom (John 16:13).
- **Convict and transform hearts** – He brings conviction of sin and enables believers to live in righteousness (John 16:8).
- **Empower boldness in witnessing** – The apostles, once fearful, became bold preachers after receiving the Holy Spirit (Acts 4:31).

**Speaking in Tongues: A Heavenly Language**

One of the manifestations of the Holy Spirit's power is speaking in tongues, also known as praying in the Spirit. This supernatural gift was first demonstrated on the Day of Pentecost:

*"And they were all filled with the Holy Ghost, and began to speak with other tongues, as the Spirit gave them utterance."* (Acts 2:4)

Speaking in tongues serves multiple purposes:

1. **A Sign of the Baptism of the Holy Spirit**
    - In Acts 10:44-46, when the Gentiles received the Holy Spirit, they immediately spoke in tongues.
    - It is a sign of being filled with the Spirit but not the only evidence (Galatians 5:22-23 shows the fruit of the Spirit).
2. **A Personal Prayer Language**
    - *"For he that speaketh in an unknown tongue speaketh not unto men, but unto God: for no man understandeth him; howbeit in the spirit he speaketh mysteries."* (1 Corinthians 14:2)
    - When we pray in tongues, our spirit communicates directly with God beyond our human understanding.
3. **A Weapon of Spiritual Warfare**
    - Praying in tongues strengthens the believer and helps in spiritual battles (Ephesians 6:18).

- o It builds up and edifies the spirit, bringing supernatural strength (Jude 1:20).

4. **Intercession Beyond Human Knowledge**
   - o *"Likewise the Spirit also helpeth our infirmities: for we know not what we should pray for as we ought: but the Spirit itself maketh intercession for us with groanings which cannot be uttered."* (Romans 8:26)
   - o When we do not know what to pray, the Holy Spirit intercedes through us, praying according to God's perfect will.

**Receiving the Gift of the Holy Spirit and Tongues**

Every believer can receive the baptism of the Holy Spirit with the evidence of speaking in tongues. Here's how:

1. **Desire and Ask for It** – *"If ye then, being evil, know how to give good gifts unto your children: how much more shall your heavenly Father give the Holy Spirit to them that ask him?"* (Luke 11:13)
2. **Believe and Receive by Faith** – Just as salvation is received by faith, so is the baptism of the Holy Spirit.
3. **Yield to the Holy Spirit** – Speaking in tongues requires yielding, allowing the Holy Spirit to move through you.
4. **Continue to Grow in It** – The more you pray in tongues, the stronger your spirit becomes, and the more you operate in the power of the Holy Spirit.

The Holy Spirit is the greatest gift God has given to believers for empowerment, guidance and transformation. Speaking in tongues is a powerful tool that strengthens us spiritually, deepens our intimacy with God, and equips us for victorious living. When you walk in the fullness of the Holy Spirit, you walk in supernatural power.

**An Encouragement for Those Battling with Receiving the Holy Spirit and Boldness**

If you are battling with receiving the Holy Spirit and the boldness to live out your faith, I want you to know you are not alone. The journey to receiving the fullness of the Holy Spirit can sometimes feel long, uncertain, and even discouraging. But I want to remind you that God sees you, He knows your heart, and He has a perfect plan for your life.

The desire to be filled with the Holy Spirit is a beautiful thing. It is a longing for a deeper connection with God, for the empowerment to live the life He has called you to. It is natural to feel a little confused or even doubtful at times, especially when others around you seem to be experiencing what you are seeking. But do not let that discourage you. The Holy Spirit is a gift, and God will fill you in His perfect timing. His timing is not limited by our expectations, but it is always right on time, just when you need it the most.

I know it can be frustrating to feel like you are still waiting, still longing, and still pressing in for that breakthrough. But I want to encourage you to hold on to your faith. Keep seeking, keep praying, and keep asking. God is a loving Father who wants to give good gifts to His children, and the Holy Spirit is one of the greatest gifts He has for you.

As you wait for this incredible experience, trust that God is preparing you. He is preparing your heart to receive the fullness of His Spirit. There may be things in your life that need to be aligned, areas where He's refining you, and things He's teaching you as you wait. Even in the waiting, God is at work.

Receiving the Holy Spirit is not just about the moment of filling—it is about a continual relationship with Him. The Holy Spirit empowers you to live boldly, to share the Gospel, and to overcome the fears and doubts that may be holding you back. If you are battling with receiving boldness, I want to remind you that the Holy Spirit gives you courage to step out in faith, even when fear tries to grip you.

When the Holy Spirit fills you, He does not just give you boldness for a moment—He transforms you. He gives you a new strength, a new fire, and a new sense of purpose. The same power that raised Jesus from the dead dwells in you, and that power equips you to live confidently and boldly for God. Fear may try to rise up, but with the Holy Spirit inside you, you can overcome it. As you step out in obedience and faith, God will continue to strengthen you and give you the boldness to preach His Word, to speak truth, and to live for Him without fear.

I want to encourage you to keep pressing forward. Do not give up on your hunger for the Holy Spirit. Keep seeking, keep asking, and keep believing. And remember, you do not have to have it all figured out—God is not looking for perfection. He is looking for a willing heart. Trust in His perfect timing. He will fill you, and when He does, it will change everything.

Until that moment comes, hold on to the promise that God is with you, and He is faithfully preparing you for what He has ahead. Be bold in your faith, keep pursuing Him, and know that the Holy Spirit will empower you in ways you never imagined. You are never alone on this journey, and God will give you the boldness to live the life He has called you to. Keep pressing in—your breakthrough is on the way.

**Spirit of Doubt**

The demonic spirit of doubt is a subtle but destructive force designed to weaken a believer's faith and trust in God. It thrives on fear, confusion, and past disappointments, planting seeds of unbelief that challenge the promises and Word of God. This spirit often whispers lies, much like Satan did in the Garden of Eden, asking, *"Did God really say?"* to distort truth and breed uncertainty. Doubt can hinder prayers, block breakthroughs, and lead to double-mindedness, making it difficult to move forward in faith. However, through meditating on Scripture, praying for increased faith, rebuking the spirit of doubt, and standing firm in the promises of God, believers can overcome its influence. Worship and fellowship with faith-filled individuals further strengthen spiritual resilience, reminding us that with God, all things are possible. When faith is activated, doubt loses its power, and believers can walk boldly in the fullness of God's purpose.

**Message of Hope**

To those discouraged about not speaking in tongues, know that God's love for you is not defined by the manifestation of the Holy Spirit in any particular way. The Bible tells us that the Holy Spirit is with all believers, filling them with His presence and guiding them in every step of their walk with God. If speaking in tongues has not come to you yet, do not be discouraged. It is a beautiful gift, but not the only measure of the Holy Spirit's work in your life.

Remember, the Spirit is at work in you in many ways—through peace, joy, patience, love and faithfulness. He equips you for service and strengthens you to live a godly life. Trust in God's timing, knowing that He gives gifts according to His will. Sometimes, the journey of seeking Him is just as important as the gifts themselves.

Keep seeking Him with a humble and open heart, and know that the Holy Spirit is always with you, guiding you and empowering you in ways that are beyond your understanding. His presence is a constant source of comfort and strength. Rest in the assurance that you are loved, chosen and equipped for every good work He has planned for you. Keep pressing forward, for He will meet you exactly where you are, and in His perfect timing, He will bring new revelations of His power into your life.

**Declarations**

I declare that I am a child of God, filled with the Holy Spirit, who empowers me to live a life of victory, peace and purpose. The Spirit of God dwells within me, guiding me with wisdom, filling me with strength, and comforting me in every season of life. I trust God's timing is perfect, and I believe His plans for me are good. I declare that fear, doubt and discouragement have no place in my life, for I walk by faith, knowing that the Holy Spirit equips me to overcome every obstacle. I embrace the gifts of the Spirit, and I know He is working in me and through me to fulfill His purpose. I am filled with hope, knowing that God's promises are yes and amen, and I will see His hand move in my life in ways that bring glory to His name. I stand firm in the truth that I am loved, chosen and equipped for every good work He has prepared for me. I declare that nothing can separate me from the love of God, and I trust that He is always with me, guiding me by His Spirit every step of the way.

# Testimony #5
# Deliverance

**John 8:36 KJV**
*"If the Son therefore shall make you free, ye shall be free indeed."*

Many people hear the word *deliverance* and immediately think of exorcisms, casting out demons, or supernatural encounters. While deliverance can involve those aspects, it is much more than that. Deliverance is the process of being set free—spiritually, emotionally, and sometimes even physically—from the bondage that keeps us from fully walking in the freedom Christ has given us. It is a divine rescue mission orchestrated by God to remove the chains of oppression, addiction, fear, sin, and anything else that hinders our spiritual growth and relationship with Him.

Deliverance is about liberation. It is the act of being released from strongholds that have kept us bound, whether they stem from generational curses, past traumas, sinful habits, or demonic oppression. The Bible tells us in John 8:36, *"So if the Son sets you free, you will be free indeed."* This means deliverance is not just an event but a process of walking in the freedom Christ has already made available to us through His death and resurrection.

When I accepted Jesus Christ in 2011, I thought that was the moment everything would change instantly. And in many ways, it did. I was saved—I knew I belonged to Christ, and I experienced His love in a way I never had before. But salvation and deliverance are not always the same thing. While salvation is the moment we are justified before God and granted eternal life through faith in Jesus, deliverance is the ongoing journey of being made whole.

Even after accepting Jesus, there were still things in my life I needed to be free from. My apostle prayed for me for many years, believing for my complete deliverance. It was discouraging at times because I would think I was free, but then still needed more prayer. There were moments when I questioned God—wondering why deliverance was taking so long. There were times I wanted to give up, but I pressed on.

One day, during a season of fasting and prayer, I cried out to God with all my heart. My apostle prayed a simple prayer, as the LORD directed, and in that moment, I felt so different. Something shifted. It was then that I realized God does not always answer when or how we expect, but He always answers. The devil fights hard to keep those who have great purpose in bondage, but he cannot stand against the power of God.

Many believers struggle after salvation because they assume that once they accept Christ, all their struggles will immediately disappear. But deliverance is often a process that requires faith, obedience and surrender to God.

For me, deliverance was something I had to walk through step by step. I still faced battles—fears, insecurities and struggles that needed to be broken off my life. God had to heal deep wounds, renew my mind, and remove strongholds that had been built over years. The LORD was not just interested in saving my soul but in setting me free completely.

**Do Christians Need Deliverance?**

The concept of Christians being demonized refers to the reality that while believers in Christ cannot be possessed by demons due to the indwelling of the Holy Spirit, they can still experience spiritual oppression, attacks, or demonic influence in their lives. This can manifest as strongholds of fear, addiction, anxiety, confusion, depression, anger, or persistent temptation. Demonization is when these forces exert control over certain areas of a believer's life, but they do not possess the believer's soul or spirit, as they are sealed by the Holy Spirit.

**Demonization**

The term *demonization* refers to various levels of demonic influence on a person. It does not always mean full possession but can include oppression, influence or strongholds that affect a believer's life. While a born-again Christian cannot be *possessed* (fully controlled) by a demon since the Holy Spirit dwells in them (1 Corinthians 6:19), they can experience **demonic oppression**— a form of external pressure or internal strongholds.

**How Christians Can Experience Demonization**

Here are some ways a Christian can open doors to demonic influence:

A. Unrepented Sin

- **Ephesians 4:26-27** warns, *"Be angry, and do not sin; do not let the sun go down on your wrath, nor give place to the devil."* Unrepented sin—especially habitual sin—gives Satan a foothold.
- Sins like unforgiveness, sexual immorality, hatred, and pride can create spiritual openings.

B. Involvement in the Occult or Witchcraft

- Practices such as astrology, tarot cards, divination, and consulting mediums invite demonic influence (Deuteronomy 18:10-12).
- Even seemingly harmless activities (e.g., horoscopes, New Age meditation) can expose believers to demonic deception.

C. Generational Curses and Family History

- Exodus 20:5 speaks of sins affecting generations. While Jesus redeems believers from the curse of the law (Galatians 3:13), generational patterns of sin can create openings if not renounced.

D. Trauma and Emotional Wounds

- Deep emotional wounds, rejection, and abuse can become entry points for demonic oppression.
- Bitterness and inner vows (e.g., "I will never trust again.") can reinforce strongholds.

E. Ungodly Soul Ties

- Relationships formed through sexual sin or deep emotional bonds outside of God's will can create demonic connections (1 Corinthians 6:16).
- These ties may need to be broken through prayer and repentance.

F. False Doctrines and Deception

- 1 Timothy 4:1 warns that some will depart from the faith, giving heed to *"deceiving spirits and doctrines of demons."* Engaging with false teachings or rejecting biblical truth can invite deception.

Signs of Demonic Influence in a Christian's Life

While discernment and prayer are needed, some indicators of demonic influence may include:

- **Persistent sinful thoughts or temptations** that feel uncontrollable.

- **Unusual fear, depression, or torment** that is spiritual in nature.
- **Difficulty praying or reading the Bible**, with strong resistance to spiritual disciplines.
- **Hearing voices or intrusive thoughts** urging self-harm or sin.
- **Addictions or compulsive behaviors** that seem beyond natural willpower.

## Deliverance from Sinful Bondages

Sin creates an open door for the enemy to operate in a person's life. While everyone struggles with sin at times, habitual or unrepented sin can lead to spiritual captivity. Some common strongholds include:

- **Sexual Immorality:** Fornication, adultery, pornography, masturbation, and homosexuality (1 Corinthians 6:18).
- **Addictions:** Substance abuse, alcoholism, nicotine, gambling, and compulsive spending (Galatians 5:19-21).
- **Gluttony and Overeating:** An unhealthy relationship with food that controls a person's emotions and physical health (Proverbs 23:2).
- **Lying and Deception:** A lifestyle of dishonesty, whether in relationships, finances, or self-representation (Colossians 3:9).

Sinful bondages may start small but can develop into strongholds, making it difficult to break free without spiritual intervention. True deliverance comes through repentance, renouncing sin, and relying on the power of the Holy Spirit.

## Deliverance from Occult and Witchcraft

Many people unknowingly invite demonic forces into their lives by engaging in occult practices. These activities may seem harmless or entertaining at first, but they create spiritual agreements with darkness:

- **Divination:** Horoscopes, astrology, tarot cards, psychic readings, Ouija boards (Deuteronomy 18:10-12).
- **Witchcraft & Sorcery:** Spells, voodoo, energy healing, New Age practices, Wicca, and Reiki (Galatians 5:20).
- **False Religions & Secret Societies:** False religion is any belief system or faith that does not align with the teachings of Jesus Christ and the Bible. Secret societies are organizations that operate with hidden or exclusive memberships, rituals, and purposes. (John 14:6).
- **Ancestral Worship & Cultural Rituals:** Practices that venerate ancestors or involve rituals apart from God's Word (Leviticus 19:31).

When people open doors to the occult, they often experience spiritual oppression, nightmares, mental torment, or unexplained struggles in their lives. Deliverance requires renouncing these practices, destroying occult objects, and seeking prayer and guidance from mature believers.

**Deliverance from Emotional and Mental Strongholds**

Not all struggles are physical—many are spiritual battles of the mind and heart. The enemy attacks people's emotions, trying to keep them bound in fear, depression or brokenness:

- **Fear and Anxiety:** Constant worry, panic attacks, or irrational fears (2 Timothy 1:7).
- **Depression and Suicidal Thoughts:** A heavy spirit of despair, hopelessness, and self-harm tendencies (Psalm 34:17-18).

- **Unforgiveness and Bitterness:** Holding onto past hurts and refusing to forgive (Matthew 6:14-15).
- **Anger and Rage:** Uncontrollable anger leading to conflict and destruction (Ephesians 4:26-27).
- **Low Self-Esteem and Insecurity:** Feelings of worthlessness, comparison, and self-rejection (Psalm 139:14).

The mind is a battlefield, and many people suffer from strongholds that distort their identity and keep them from experiencing God's peace. Deliverance comes by renewing the mind with the Word of God and breaking agreement with lies from the enemy.

**Deliverance from Generational Curses**

Some struggles are passed down through family bloodlines. These patterns may appear as generational cycles of sin, sickness or failure:

- **Poverty and Financial Struggles:** Recurring financial hardship despite efforts to break free (Deuteronomy 28:15-68).
- **Family Dysfunction:** Divorce, abuse, broken marriages, and rebellious children (Malachi 2:16).
- **Sickness and Premature Death:** Recurring diseases or early deaths in family history (Exodus 20:5).
- **Addiction and Bondage:** Generational alcoholism, drug use, or other addictive behaviors (Numbers 14:18).

The blood of Jesus breaks every curse (Galatians 3:13). Through prayer, repentance, and faith in Christ's finished work, believers can break free from inherited patterns.

**Deliverance from Spirit Spouses and Unholy Soul Ties**

Many people suffer from spiritual relationships they are unaware of. These bonds can interfere with relationships, cause marital struggles, or block spiritual growth:

- **Spirit Spouses:** Sexual encounters in dreams, sleep paralysis, and unexplained relationship difficulties.
- **Unholy Soul Ties:** Sexual or emotional connections with past partners that negatively affect a person's mind and emotions (1 Corinthians 6:16).
- **Toxic Relationships:** Strong attachments to manipulative or abusive individuals that prevent spiritual progress.

Breaking soul ties requires renouncing past relationships, asking God to cleanse the heart, and cutting off ungodly emotional or spiritual bonds.

**Deliverance from the Spirit of Death and Suicide**

The enemy seeks to steal, kill and destroy (John 10:10). Many suffer under a spirit of death, which manifests in:

- **Suicidal thoughts or self-harm urges.**
- **Chronic illnesses and diseases that will not heal.**
- **Attraction to dark, gothic, or death-related themes.**

Deliverance from the spirit of death involves breaking agreement with thoughts of hopelessness and declaring life in Jesus' name. Speaking God's Word over one's life brings healing and restoration.

Deliverance from the Jezebel Spirit and Control

The Jezebel spirit operates through manipulation, seduction and rebellion. Signs of this spirit include:

- **Controlling or manipulative behavior in relationships.**

- **Sexual seduction or using sex for power.**
- **Rebellion against God-ordained authority.**

This spirit can influence individuals, families, and even churches. Deliverance involves repentance, humility and submission to God's authority.

**Deliverance from Financial Bondage**

Many people are bound in cycles of lack and financial struggle:

- **Debt and never getting ahead.**
- **Poor financial stewardship and wastefulness.**
- **A poverty mindset that limits faith in God's provision.**

Deliverance from financial bondage involves seeking wisdom, practicing biblical principles of giving, and breaking any spiritual chains holding back prosperity (Malachi 3:10-11). There are countless spirits from which one may need deliverance. These are just a few.

**How Christians Can Overcome and Stay Free**

If a believer is experiencing demonic oppression, they can be set free through biblical means:

A. Genuine Repentance and Confession

- 1 John 1:9, *"If we confess our sins, He is faithful and just to forgive us our sins and to cleanse us from all unrighteousness."*
- Renouncing any sinful behavior or involvement in darkness.

B. Breaking Legal Rights of the Enemy

- Renounce any ties to sin, occult involvement, or ungodly soul ties.
- Declare freedom in Christ (Galatians 5:1).

C. Deliverance Through the Authority of Jesus

- Jesus gave believers power over demonic forces (Luke 10:19, Mark 16:17).
- Deliverance may involve fasting, prayer, and seeking the help of mature believers or church leaders.

D. Filling the House with God's Presence

- After deliverance, a believer must stay filled with the Holy Spirit and renew their mind (Matthew 12:43-45, Romans 12:2).
- Daily prayer, worship, and Scripture study strengthen spiritual defenses.

E. Putting on the Armor of God

- Ephesians 6:10-18 instructs believers to put on the full armor of God, including truth, righteousness, faith, and the Word of God, to stand against the enemy's schemes.

**Walking in Freedom**

Deliverance is not just about breaking free—it is about staying free. Jesus taught that when a demon is cast out, it seeks to return (Matthew 12:43-45). True deliverance requires:

1. A personal relationship with Jesus Christ.
2. Daily prayer, fasting, and reading the Word.
3. Breaking ungodly agreements and renouncing sin.
4. Walking in holiness and obedience to God.
5. Surrounding oneself with strong, Spirit-filled believers.

Jesus came to set the captives free, and true freedom is found in Him alone. Whatever you may need deliverance from, know that God is mighty to save. The blood of Jesus is enough to break every chain!

God's deliverance is available to everyone who seeks it. No matter what stronghold or bondage you may be facing, God is more than able to set you free. Keep seeking, keep believing, and receive the deliverance that Jesus has already won for you on the cross.

**Message of Hope**

No matter the chains that bind you, no matter the struggles that weigh heavy on your heart, know that deliverance is available to you through the power of Jesus Christ. He came to set the captives free and to bring healing to the brokenhearted. Whatever you are facing—whether it is addiction, fear, oppression, or past trauma—there is freedom in His name.

Jesus has already won the victory, and through Him, you are empowered to overcome every stronghold. The Holy Spirit is at work in you, renewing your mind, healing your wounds, and breaking the chains that have held you back. You are not defined by your past or by the struggles you face. You are a new creation in Christ, and He has a plan for your life that is full of hope, peace and purpose.

Take courage, for deliverance is not a distant promise—it is a present reality. Stand firm in your faith, trusting in the power of God's Word and His promises. The deliverance you seek is found in His presence, in the blood of Jesus, and in the power of the Holy Spirit. As you call on His name, you will find the strength to rise above every obstacle, knowing that God is with you, fighting on your behalf.

You are free in Christ, and His deliverance is the path to your peace and restoration. Hold fast to His promises, for He who began a good work in you will carry it to completion.

**Declaration**

I declare that I am free in the name of Jesus Christ. Every chain, every stronghold, and every spirit of oppression must bow to the authority of Christ. I am no longer bound by fear, addiction, past trauma, or any form of bondage, for Jesus has set me free. The blood of Jesus has washed me clean, and I stand in the victory that He has already won on the cross. I declare that I am a new creation in Christ, and I walk in the freedom that He has provided.

I declare that every lie of the enemy is broken, and I refuse to accept anything that contradicts the truth of God's Word. I claim the fullness of His deliverance in my life. The Holy Spirit is my guide, my comforter, and my strength, and He empowers me to overcome every obstacle. I speak life and victory over my mind, body and spirit. Every area of my life is restored by the power of God's love and grace.

I declare that no weapon formed against me shall prosper. I am covered by the blood of Jesus, and the enemy has no authority over my life. I walk in the freedom that God has promised, and I will not be held captive by anything that does not align with His will. I am delivered, healed and whole in Christ, and I will testify of His goodness and power in my life.

# Testimony #6
# Bound by Love, Blessed by God

**Mark 10:9 KJV**

*"What therefore God hath joined together, let not man put asunder."*

My husband and I first met in church, where we both served in the youth ministry. At that time, there were no romantic feelings between us. Our connection was purely one of mutual respect and shared purpose. Together, we worked to uplift and guide the younger generation, forging a partnership grounded in faith and service. Little did we know, God had a greater plan for our lives.

Our journey toward marriage began with a profound revelation from God. For me, it started with a dream, which was soon followed by a vision that left me in awe. At the same time, my husband experienced a vision of his own, confirming what God had revealed to me. We were both shocked and unsure of what to make of it initially, but the clarity of these revelations was undeniable. It became clear that God had chosen us for each other.

Filled with excitement and a sense of divine purpose, we decided to share the news with our families. My husband's family was ecstatic; their joy and support were immediate and unwavering. However, my family's reaction was quite different. Despite the fact that we both shared Guyanese heritage, the cultural differences between us presented a significant challenge. My husband is of Afro-Guyanese descent, while I am Indo-Guyanese. This distinction led to disapproval from my family. They were concerned about the cultural differences and how it might impact our future together.

In the face of this disapproval, my husband and I turned to God. We believed that if He had ordained our union, He would also make a way for us. We prayed fervently for guidance, strength, and for the hearts of my family to soften. It was not an easy journey. There were moments of doubt and frustration, but our faith remained steadfast.

One day, during a church service, we received a prophetic word. The message was clear. It was time for us to be joined together in marriage. This confirmation from God reassured us and gave us the courage to move forward, trusting Him to handle the obstacles in our path.

Despite the initial resistance, God worked in miraculous ways to bring us together. Slowly but surely, we saw hearts begin to change, and circumstances shift in our favor. On the day of our wedding, it was evident that our union was not just a celebration of love but also a testimony to God's faithfulness. He had orchestrated every detail, proving that with Him, all things are possible.

Our marriage has been rooted in the foundation of faith and trust in God. The challenges we faced before our union served to strengthen our bond and remind us of the importance of putting God at the center of our relationship. Today, as we reflect on our journey, we are grateful for the lessons learned and the love that continues to grow between us.

Marriage is more than just a union between two people; it is a covenant that reflects God's love and purpose. Our story is a reminder that when God brings two people together, no obstacle is too great to overcome.

If you are facing a situation where your marriage is not yet approved, whether by family, community, or authorities, take heart in knowing that God sees your heart and knows the desires of your soul. The journey you are on may be challenging, but God is faithful, and He has a plan for your life and your relationship. In times of uncertainty, trust that His timing is perfect, and His ways are higher than our ways.

**God Chooses Your Soulmate**

The concept of a soulmate is often romanticized in popular culture, but for the Christian, the idea goes deeper. God, in His infinite wisdom and love, has a plan for each of our lives, and that includes the person He has chosen for us to walk through life with in marriage. A soulmate, in this sense, is not just someone with whom you have chemistry or share common interests, but someone whom God has intentionally brought into your life to fulfill a higher purpose.

In Scripture, we see the hand of God in the formation of relationships. In Genesis, when God created Eve, He saw that Adam was alone and said, *"It is not good for the man to be alone. I will make a helper suitable for him"* (Genesis 2:18). God did not leave Adam to figure things out on his own. He carefully and purposefully designed Eve to be his companion, just as God, in His perfect timing, designs the right partner for each of us.

Trusting that God has chosen your soulmate means surrendering your desires and expectations to Him. It is recognizing that His timing, wisdom, and plans are far greater than our own. While we might wish for a particular type of person or idealize the perfect partner, God knows what we truly need. He understands our strengths, weaknesses, and unique calling, and He knows exactly who will complement us in fulfilling His purpose for our lives. A soulmate chosen by God is someone who will support you spiritually, emotionally, and mentally, and together, you will help each other grow closer to God.

God does not just choose someone who makes us feel good in the moment or checks all the boxes of what we think we need in a partner. He chooses someone who will challenge us, refine us, and help us become the people He created us to be. A soulmate is someone who will encourage us in our faith, stand with us through trials, and walk beside us in the journey of life.

The process of finding your soulmate is a journey of faith, patience and trust. It requires surrendering to God's will and trusting that He knows what is best for us, even when the road ahead seems uncertain. In waiting for God's timing, we learn to grow in character, to become the right partner ourselves, and to align our desires with God's purpose for our lives. And when God brings your soulmate into your life, you will see His faithfulness and love in a way that only a divinely orchestrated relationship can reveal.

When you embrace the idea that God has chosen your soulmate, it brings peace and assurance. No longer do you have to worry about whether you made the *right* choice or if the relationship will last. Knowing that God is at the center of it all allows you to focus on building a Christ-centered partnership, one where both individuals are committed to loving God and each other, growing together, and fulfilling the purpose God has for their marriage.

Ultimately, God's choice of your soulmate is a reflection of His perfect love and divine provision. It is a beautiful reminder that God is in control, He knows your heart, and He has an incredible plan to bring you together with the one who will walk beside you in life, sharing the joy and challenges of the journey as partners in His kingdom.

## Marriage is Ministry

Marriage is more than a union between two people. It is a divine ministry; a sacred calling. God designed marriage as an institution to reflect His love, grace and purpose in the world. It is not merely a relationship to fulfill personal desires or needs but a partnership in which each spouse plays a role in fulfilling God's plan for their lives, their family, and the world around them.

At its core, marriage is ministry because it requires selflessness, sacrifice, and a deep commitment to loving and serving one another. Ephesians 5:25 reminds husbands to *"love your wives, just as Christ loved the church and gave Himself up for her."* This sacrificial love mirrors the ministry of Christ, who gave His life for the church, and in the same way, husbands are called to lay down their own desires for the sake of their wives.

Likewise, wives are called to embrace a ministry of support, respect and encouragement, as the Bible teaches in Ephesians 5:33, *"Let the wife see that she respects her husband."* The marriage relationship, when viewed through the lens of ministry, becomes one of mutual service, where both partners strive to lift each other up in their faith, encouraging each other to grow in their walk with God. The couple becomes a reflection of God's love, grace and mercy to the world.

Marriage also serves as a ministry to the family. Children observe the relationship between their parents and learn what love, respect and partnership look like. Parents have the responsibility to model godly relationships, to nurture their children in faith, and to teach them how to build relationships that honor God. The home, when grounded in God's Word, becomes a sanctuary where love is cultivated, and spiritual growth flourishes.

Furthermore, marriage as ministry extends beyond the home. Couples who view their marriage as a ministry have the opportunity to impact their church, their community, and even the world. They can serve together in ministry roles, whether in outreach programs, helping others, or supporting their church's vision. When two individuals are united in Christ, their combined strength and resources can multiply their impact in ways they could not accomplish alone.

Through the challenges and triumphs that marriage brings, God works within the relationship to refine each spouse, teaching them patience, humility, forgiveness, and unconditional love. Marriage becomes a powerful ministry not because it is perfect, but because it reflects the ongoing work of God in the lives of His people.

Ultimately, when couples embrace their marriage as a ministry, they allow God to use their relationship to fulfill His purposes on earth. Their union becomes a living testimony of His love, a beacon of hope to a world in need of His grace, and a reminder that, through Christ, all things are possible.

To overcome division and stand strong in a Christ-centered marriage, couples must be proactive in guarding their relationship and their faith. Here are several steps to help combat the devil's tactics and strengthen the bond between spouses:

1.  **Pray Together:** One of the most powerful tools to protect a marriage is prayer. Couples who pray together build a spiritual foundation that keeps them close to each other and to God. Prayer opens the door for God's guidance, peace and protection. It helps to align both partners' hearts toward God's will and reminds them that they are not fighting against each other, but against spiritual forces that seek to destroy their unity.

2. **Build Trust and Communication:** Communication is key in any relationship, but in a marriage, it is essential. Open, honest conversations can prevent misunderstandings and offer opportunities for reconciliation when conflicts arise. Trust is also crucial, as it allows both spouses to feel safe, loved and supported. When a couple is united in trust and clear communication, it becomes more difficult for the devil to cause division.

3. **Put God First:** In a Christ-centered marriage, God must be the foundation. Both spouses should prioritize their individual relationship with God, seeking His will for their lives. A strong personal relationship with God enables both partners to serve each other with love and humility. When God is first in a marriage, the couple can withstand the storms of life together, knowing that their bond is anchored in Him.

4. **Practice Forgiveness:** Forgiveness is a powerful tool that can help a couple heal from hurt and disappointment. The devil thrives on bitterness, resentment and unforgiveness, but through Christ, couples are called to forgive as they have been forgiven. By choosing forgiveness, couples can release the grip of division and move forward in peace and unity.

5. **Support Each Other in Faith:** It is important for couples to support each other in their spiritual journeys. Encouraging one another in the faith strengthens the marriage and helps both partners grow in their walk with God. When both spouses are growing spiritually, they are more equipped to handle challenges and face them together.

6. **Remember the Purpose of Marriage:** Marriage, as ordained by God, has a divine purpose. It is not just about companionship or shared responsibilities. It is about reflecting the love of Christ to the world. Couples should remind themselves of this purpose, keeping in mind that their marriage is a testimony of God's love and grace. When they

see their marriage in this light, they are less likely to allow division to take root.

## Spirit of Division

The spirit of division is a destructive force that seeks to break unity and create separation, discord and strife among individuals, families, communities, and even within the body of Christ. It is a spirit that thrives on misunderstanding, miscommunication and unforgiveness. It works quietly but powerfully, often using subtle tactics to plant seeds of bitterness, resentment and jealousy. The Bible warns us against division, urging believers to guard against anything that disrupts harmony and peace within relationships.

In Scripture, we see the destructive effects of division. In 1 Corinthians 1:10, the apostle Paul urges the church to be united. *"I appeal to you, brothers and sisters, in the name of our Lord Jesus Christ, that all of you agree with one another in what you say and that there be no divisions among you, but that you be perfectly united in mind and thought."* Paul understood the power of unity and the danger that division could bring to the body of Christ. When division takes root, it weakens the church, undermines the message of the Gospel, and prevents believers from fully experiencing the love and power of God.

The spirit of division often begins with small disagreements or differences of opinion, but when allowed to fester, it grows into a much larger problem. It thrives on gossip, criticism, and the spread of negativity. It whispers lies, convincing individuals that they are justified in their anger or hurt, and encourages them to hold grudges or take offense. Over time, the spirit of division causes walls to rise between people, relationships to break down, and communities to fracture.

One of the primary ways the spirit of division operates is through pride and self-centeredness. When individuals become more concerned with their own desires, preferences and feelings than with the well-being of others, it creates a fertile ground for division. The enemy often works to magnify small differences and blow them out of proportion, making it easy to lose sight of the bigger picture—our common faith in Christ and the calling to love one another. The enemy's goal is to divide and conquer, to isolate individuals and weaken the collective strength of the body of Christ.

However, the Bible provides clear guidance on how to combat division. Ephesians 4:3 encourages believers to *"make every effort to keep the unity of the Spirit through the bond of peace."* Unity is not something that happens automatically. It requires effort, humility and intentionality. When we choose to walk in love, to forgive, and to listen with understanding, we dismantle the power of division. As believers, we are called to be peacemakers, to reconcile differences, and to be agents of healing in relationships.

The spirit of division cannot thrive where love, humility and forgiveness reign. The Bible commands us to love one another, not only in words but also in actions. We are called to bear one another's burdens, to speak the truth in love, and to seek reconciliation whenever division arises. Jesus Himself prayed for unity among His followers in John 17:21, saying, *"That all of them may be one, Father, just as you are in me and I am in you."* Christ's desire for His church is that we be united in heart, mind and purpose, reflecting the unity that exists between Him and the Father.

When we resist the spirit of division, we allow the Spirit of God to bring healing, restoration and peace into our relationships. We become a living testimony of God's love, showing the world that, in Christ, we are one. The spirit of unity fosters growth, encouragement and strength, and it enables us to fulfill God's purpose for our lives individually and as the body of Christ.

Ultimately, the spirit of division is an enemy to the peace, harmony, and love that God desires for His people. But as believers, we are equipped to stand against it by walking in the Spirit, extending grace and forgiveness, and making every effort to maintain unity. When we do this, we allow God's love to shine through us, and we become a powerful witness to the world of His transforming grace.

Ultimately, overcoming division in a Christ-centered marriage requires intentionality, prayer, and a focus on God's design for relationships. The devil may try to create division, but with God's help, couples can overcome any obstacle. By staying rooted in their faith, being intentional with communication and love, and prioritizing God's will in their marriage, they can build a strong, lasting bond that reflects Christ's love and serves as a witness to the world.

**Message of Hope**

God values the covenant of marriage, and He is with you in this process. While approval from others is important, it does not define the strength or legitimacy of your relationship. Your marriage is between you, your spouse, and God. If you are committed to building a foundation of love, respect and faith, trust that God is honored by your commitment.

In moments of doubt or discouragement, lean into God's Word. He promises that He will never leave you nor forsake you, and that He will make a way even when it seems impossible. Stay rooted in prayer, seeking His wisdom and guidance as you navigate this season. Trust that He is working all things together for your good and His glory.

Remember, God is a God of restoration and reconciliation. If there are relationships that need healing for approval to come, trust that God can soften hearts and open doors in His perfect timing. Keep walking in faith, knowing that God's love for you and your marriage is steadfast, and He will guide you through every challenge with hope and grace. Your journey is not over, and with God by your side, your story is still being written.

**Declarations**

I declare that my identity and worth are rooted in Christ, not in the approval or opinions of others. Though I may not have the approval I desire from those around me regarding my marriage, I trust God's plan for my life is perfect and His timing is always right. I know God is the ultimate source of validation, and He has brought me and my spouse together according to His will. I stand firm in the knowledge that God is guiding our relationship and will provide everything we need to thrive in love and unity.

I declare that my relationship is founded on God's love, truth and purpose. No matter the challenges or the lack of approval from others, I will not be shaken, for I know God is with me and has already established the covenant of my marriage. I trust in His ability to soften hearts, open doors, and bring peace to those who may not yet understand His plan for us.

I choose to honor God in my marriage, regardless of the opinions of others, and I trust that He will work all things together for our good. I will walk in peace, confidence and patience, knowing that God is working in and through our marriage for His glory. I declare that no external disapproval will hinder the purpose and blessings God has for our union. We are secure in God's love and plan, and we trust that He will bring about healing, understanding and reconciliation in His perfect time.

# Testimony #7
# Birth Blessings

**Luke 1:37 KJV**
*"For with God nothing shall be impossible."*

Becoming a mother is a sacred journey, one filled with joy, anticipation and challenges that shape the way you view life. My journey through childbirth was not what I had imagined, but in hindsight, I can see how God's hand was all over it. His plan for my family was greater than my own, and it was a testimony of His faithfulness, power and grace.

## Firstborn – The Unexpected Turn

When I first found out I was pregnant with my son, I was ecstatic. This was the beginning of a new chapter, and I had dreams and visions of how it would all unfold. I imagined a smooth, natural delivery where I could experience the excitement of bringing my child into the world in a peaceful way. But as we all know, life does not always go as planned.

The day came for the doctor to induce my labor. I had reached the end of my pregnancy, and it was time for my son to be born. Everything started out as expected. I was in the hospital, ready to welcome my baby. The labor pains began to intensify, and I was progressing. At one point, I reached 8 centimeters dilated, and I thought to myself, *"It's almost time!"*

But as the hours passed, something went wrong. The doctor came in, monitoring my son's heart rate, and he noticed it was dropping. His condition was concerning, and in that moment, everything changed. Without hesitation, the doctor made the decision for an emergency C-section.

I was filled with a mixture of emotions—fear, confusion, and even disappointment. The birth I had planned for my son was slipping away, and I found myself in a whirlwind of medical staff rushing around. The pressure to make the right decisions and the realization that my body was not responding as expected weighed heavily on me.

In that moment, I realized that while I had planned for one thing, God had another plan. I knew that His hand was on me, guiding me through the unexpected turn of events. In His sovereignty, He allowed the doctors to intervene, and my son was safely delivered via emergency C-section.

**The Recovery Process – A Time of Reflection**

The days that followed were not easy. Recovering from an emergency C-section was a lengthy process, both physically and emotionally. I remember the pain, the discomfort, and the frustration that came with the healing. I could not help but reflect on how things had turned out differently than I had envisioned. The emotional toll of not having the birth I had hoped for lingered, and I wondered if I could ever go through something like that again.

I even found myself questioning whether I wanted to have more children. The idea of going through another C-section, with the possibility of another emergency procedure, was daunting. I was filled with fear and uncertainty about the future. Would I be able to endure it again? What if things did not go according to plan once more?

But through it all, God was present. Even in the midst of the pain and the questions, I felt His peace. I felt the gentle reminder that His plans were still good, even when I did not understand them. I learned to trust Him more deeply, knowing that He was in control, even in the moments when I could not see the full picture.

**The Unexpected Surprise – A Gift from God**

Almost a year later, when I least expected it, I found out I was pregnant again. This time, it was a complete surprise, but I knew it was a surprise that only God could orchestrate. My husband and I had discussed the possibility of having more children, but this pregnancy came at a time when we had thought it might not happen again so soon.

The news was a mixture of joy, excitement, and a bit of apprehension. I could not help but think back to my first birth experience and the challenges I had faced. Would I be able to have a different kind of birth this time? Could I experience the natural delivery I had longed for? Would I face another C-section? These thoughts filled my mind as I went through the pregnancy, but I knew deep down that God had a plan, and I trusted Him.

As the pregnancy progressed, I found myself leaning into God more than ever before. My apostle and the church surrounded me in prayer, lifting me up in faith for a vaginal delivery. I knew this was a big request, but I also knew that with God, nothing was impossible. We prayed, we believed, and we trusted that He could make a way where there seemed to be no way.

**A Supernatural Birth – God's Faithfulness**

The day of delivery arrived, and I was filled with both peace and expectation. I had prepared for whatever God would do, but I also believed He was going to answer the prayers that had been prayed over me. The day I gave birth was unlike any I had ever imagined. It was supernatural.

God spoke to me throughout the entire process. There were moments when I felt unsure - when doubt tried to creep in - but God spoke peace into my heart. I knew He was with me, and His voice was a constant reminder that I was not alone. He gave me the strength to endure and the faith to believe His plan would unfold perfectly.

And it did. Against all odds, I was able to deliver my baby vaginally. The birth was not only a miracle but a testimony of God's faithfulness to me and my family. My son was born healthy and strong, and the joy of holding him in my arms was overwhelming.

On October 30th, I heard the voice of God so clearly, *"You are going to the hospital tomorrow."* It was not a suggestion. It was a promise. I held onto those words, knowing God was guiding me through the journey ahead.

The next day, October 31st, I tried to go about my usual routine, getting things done around the house, but God interrupted my plans. *"Go shower and get prepared—it's almost time to go."* I hesitated at first, brushing off the urgency, but the voice came again, firmer this time. I obeyed, stepped into the shower, and that is when the contractions began, strong and undeniable.

We rushed to the hospital, and after being checked, I was told I was 2 centimeters dilated. It was still early, but I could feel the intensity of the moment building. The doctor came in to discuss the risks, especially given my history of a C-section. He painted a grim picture, listing everything that could go wrong—a big baby, potential complications, the possibility of the incision reopening, and the baby getting stuck. He even questioned whether I should try for a vaginal birth at all.

It was a moment that required unshakable faith. I put my trust in Jesus, refusing to let fear take hold. I knew the risks, but I also knew the One who holds life and death in His hands. I called on prayer warriors, including my apostle and others, to intercede on my behalf. Worship music filled the room, and I held onto the Word of God like an anchor in a storm.

Every time the doctor came into the room, I sensed something dark. It was not just skepticism—it felt like spiritual opposition. God revealed to me that Satan was using the doctor to bring fear and doubt into the room. But God also assured me, *"Keep praying."*

While others around me encouraged and believed, the doctor stood on the sidelines, watching with doubt. He did not think I could do it. He warned me again about the risks and even advised against trying for a vaginal birth in the future, especially with a bigger baby. But God had already spoken. He told me there were angels in the room, orchestrating every moment, and that the birth would be quick.

As the labor progressed, the promise of God unfolded just as He said it would. Though the doctor predicted it could take two to three hours, the actual delivery only took 40 minutes. God turned what seemed impossible into a testimony of His power.

Even as the doctor doubted my height, my body, and my ability to deliver naturally, God proved him wrong. The same God who told me the birth would happen around 1 a.m. brought it to pass right on time.

Through every contraction, every moment of doubt, and every attempt by the enemy to bring fear, God was faithful. He silenced the voices of doubt and intimidation and replaced them with victory.

This birth was more than just a physical process—it was a spiritual breakthrough. It was a testimony of God's power to do the impossible. Satan tried to bring fear, but faith won. The God who promises is the God who delivers, and this story is living proof of that truth.

**Reflections on God's Faithfulness**

Looking back on both experiences—the emergency C-section and the miraculous vaginal delivery—I see the hand of God in every detail. Through my first experience, God taught me about trust, surrender, and the beauty of His perfect timing. Through my second experience, He showed me that He can do the impossible and that when we place our faith in Him, He will always come through.

I now know that childbirth, like life itself, is unpredictable. Sometimes things do not go according to our plans, but God's plans are always better. He knows what we need, when we need it, and how to bring about His perfect will in our lives. Whether through a C-section or a natural birth, God is always with us, and His power is made perfect in our weakness.

As I reflect on my two births, I am filled with gratitude and awe. I am grateful for the lessons learned, the prayers answered, and the unwavering faithfulness of God. The journey of motherhood is never easy, but it is always worth it. And through it all, God is the faithful one who carries us through every challenge, every fear, and every triumph.

If you are in the midst of a challenge or an uncertainty in your life, I encourage you to lean into God. Trust that His plan for you is good. He will guide you, strengthen you, and make a way where there seems to be no way. Keep believing. Keep praying. Keep trusting. His faithfulness will never fail you.

**But God...It Does Not Make Sense**

There are times in life when the circumstances we face do not make sense. We can be doing everything right—serving God faithfully, praying, trusting Him with all our heart—and yet, things still seem to go wrong. Life feels confusing, and the confusion often leads to questions: *Why God? Why me?* It is easy to feel as though we have been forgotten or that God is somehow distant. But even when it does not make sense, we can trust that God's plan is unfolding in ways we cannot yet see.

In moments like these, it is important to remember that our understanding is limited. God's ways are higher than ours, and His wisdom transcends our human comprehension. As Ecclesiastes 11:5 reminds us, *"As thou knowest not what is the way of the spirit, nor how the bones do grow in the womb of her that is with child: even so thou knowest not the works of God who maketh all."* Just as we don't understand how life is formed in the womb, there are many things we will never fully comprehend about the way God works. It is not for us to understand everything. Our role is to trust in God's perfect plan and His timing.

Consider the story of the widow who was asked to feed the prophet Elijah with her last bit of flour and oil (1 Kings 17:8-16). It did not make sense to her, especially when she was facing a famine, yet she obeyed. When she did, God provided miraculously—her flour and oil never ran out. God does not always give us the simple answers we expect. His ways are often unpredictable, but they are always purposeful.

We often approach life like a math problem, expecting a clear and straightforward solution: $2 + 2 = 4$. But with God, His equations are different. Only He knows the answer to the complex problems we face. And because He is the answer, it is in seeking Him that we find clarity. Isaiah 55:8-9 tells us, *"For my thoughts are not your thoughts, neither are your ways my ways...For as the heavens are higher than the earth, so are my ways higher than your ways, and my thoughts than your thoughts."* While we cannot always see the end result, we can trust God knows exactly what He is doing.

Trusting God when things do not make sense requires faith. Proverbs 3:5-6 calls us to *"Trust in the Lord with all your heart and lean not on your own understanding."* It is easy to doubt or question, but faith is about surrendering our need for answers and leaning into God's wisdom, knowing He will guide us, even when we do not have all the answers right away.

There will be moments when we feel like God has forgotten us. David cried out in Psalm 13:1-3, asking, *"How long wilt thou forget me, O Lord? How long wilt thou hide thy face from me?"* Sometimes, our battles feel like they will never end, and we wonder if God is still with us. But even in those moments, God is at work. Joseph's story is a testament to this. He went from being sold by his brothers to being imprisoned, yet God had a plan to elevate him to a position where he could save many lives. What seemed like betrayal and hardship became part of God's greater purpose.

Joseph understood this truth when he later told his brothers in Genesis 50:20, *"But as for you, ye thought evil against me; but God meant it unto good, to bring to pass, as it is this day, to save much people alive."* What the enemy meant for harm, God used for good. Trusting that God is working behind the scenes—even when it does not make sense—is what strengthens our faith.

Another powerful example is found in 2 Chronicles 20, when King Jehoshaphat faced an overwhelming enemy. Instead of strategizing with conventional warfare, God told him to stand still, to sing praises, and to watch as He fought for them. As the choir marched before the army, God caused their enemies to defeat each other. What seemed illogical to the human mind was God's perfect plan in action.

In the same way, David's victory over Goliath seemed improbable. With no armor and just a slingshot, he faced a giant, yet he knew that victory did not come from human strength, but from God. What looked like a loss in the natural realm was actually God's set-up for a victory that would change history.

When it feels like God is silent or distant, He may not be revealing the entire plan right away, but He is still at work. Stay connected to Him through prayer, worship, and His Word. Listen for His voice, because He will guide you. It is in surrendering our need to understand everything that we open ourselves up to God's wisdom and direction.

Today, release the need for everything to make sense and trust God with the outcome. Let go of the confusion, the doubt, and the fear, and allow God to minister to your situation. When it feels like your world is falling apart, remember that God is not absent. His plans are perfect, and even when things do not make sense, He is working everything together for your good.

**God Doing the Impossible**

There are moments in life when we are faced with situations that seem beyond hope, beyond our ability to change, or even beyond human understanding. When we reach the limits of our own strength, resources, or understanding, we may find ourselves wondering how anything will ever work out. But God specializes in doing the impossible. He is the God who defies the laws of nature, who performs miracles that no human can explain, and who opens doors that seem firmly closed.

The Bible is full of stories where God did what seemed impossible. From the creation of the universe to the resurrection of the dead, God's ability to make the impossible possible is a theme woven throughout Scripture. His power knows no bounds, and He delights in showing us that what we think is impossible is simply an opportunity for Him to reveal His glory.

**The Impossible is Possible Through Faith**

In Matthew 17:20, Jesus told His disciples, *"If you have faith as small as a mustard seed, you can say to this mountain, 'Move from here to there,' and it will move. Nothing will be impossible for you."* This statement may sound astounding, but it underscores the principle that God works in partnership with our faith. When we trust Him, even in the face of impossibility, we allow Him to work in ways that go beyond our natural abilities.

Faith in God activates His power. It does not mean we understand *how* God will work, but it means we believe He *can and* will work, even when all signs point to the contrary. It is through faith that we see God open doors that seem closed, heal bodies that are broken, and restore relationships that seem irreparable. God's power is limitless, and when we have faith in His ability, we begin to see the impossible unfold before our eyes.

**Our Response to the Impossible**

When faced with the impossible, our response should be one of faith, trust and surrender. We may not always understand how God will work in our lives, but we can trust that He is able to do what seems impossible. We must remember that God's ways are higher than our ways (Isaiah 55:9), and His understanding is beyond our comprehension.

God calls us to walk by faith, not by sight. Even when the road ahead seems unclear or the mountain before us seems insurmountable, we can trust God will make a way. He is the God of the impossible, and He specializes in turning hopeless situations into powerful testimonies of His greatness.

When we face the impossible, we must remember nothing is too hard for God. He can turn the most hopeless situations into opportunities for His glory. And just as He has done the impossible in the past, He will continue to do so in our lives today. Our job is not to figure out how God will do it, but to believe that He will. Trust in His timing, trust in His power, and trust that He is able to do more than we could ever ask or imagine (Ephesians 3:20).

The God who parted the Red Sea, who raised the dead, who made the blind see, and who defeated death itself is the same God who works in our lives today. Whatever you are facing, no matter how impossible it seems, remember that God specializes in doing the impossible. Trust in His power, surrender to His will, and watch as He moves in ways you never thought possible. God is still doing the impossible—and He wants to do it in your life.

**Spirit of Fear**

Fear is one of the most powerful emotions that can control and manipulate a person. It has the ability to paralyze, isolate and distort our perception of reality. In its extreme form, fear becomes a spirit—a spiritual force that aims to hinder us from fulfilling our purpose, living in peace, and trusting in God's promises. The spirit of fear is not just a temporary feeling of apprehension or nervousness, but an oppressive force that tries to establish a foothold in our hearts and minds, leading us into anxiety, doubt, and even inaction.

The Bible often speaks of fear as an enemy of faith and God's perfect love. While fear is a natural human emotion, when it becomes a spirit, it goes beyond just feelings and tries to dominate our lives. The spirit of fear is not from God, and it seeks to keep us from stepping into the fullness of what God has called us to do.

**Overcoming the Spirit of Fear**

While the spirit of fear is a powerful force, God has equipped us with everything we need to overcome it. Here are some steps to break free from the spirit of fear:

1. **Recognize the Source**: The first step to overcoming fear is recognizing that it is not from God. Understanding that fear is a spirit, not a part of God's plan, helps us to resist its influence and refuse to give it control over our lives.
2. **Turn to God in Prayer**: When fear begins to take hold, turn to God in prayer. Seek His presence, and ask Him to help you overcome fear. Psalm 34:4 says, *"I sought the Lord, and He answered me; He delivered me from all my fears."* Prayer is a powerful weapon that invites God's peace into our hearts and minds.
3. **Cling to God's Promises**: Fill your mind with Scripture that counters fear. Remember that God is your protector (Psalm 91:1-2), your provider (Philippians 4:19), and your strength (Isaiah 40:29). Meditate on these promises and declare them over your life. The more we align our thinking with God's truth, the less room fear has to take hold.
4. **Take Action in Faith**: Fear paralyzes, but faith moves us forward. Even when fear whispers *"You can't do it,"* take small steps of faith toward what God has called you to. The more we act in faith, the more fear loses its power.
5. **Surround Yourself with Support**: Do not face fear alone. Surround yourself with a supportive community of believers who can pray with you, encourage you, and speak truth into

your life. Ecclesiastes 4:9-10 reminds us that *"two are better than one"* and that we are stronger together.

6. **Focus on God's Love**: 1 John 4:18 says, *"There is no fear in love. But perfect love drives out fear."* When we grasp the depth of God's love for us, fear begins to lose its grip. We can rest in the assurance that God loves us and that His love is stronger than any fear we may face.

The spirit of fear is a powerful, deceptive force that tries to control and paralyze us. But the good news is that, as believers, we do not have to live in fear. God has not given us a spirit of fear, but one of power, love, and a sound mind. By recognizing the spirit of fear for what it is, turning to God in prayer, and standing firm on His promises, we can break free from its hold and walk in the freedom and confidence that comes from trusting in God's perfect love. Fear may come, but it does not have to stay. Through Christ, we are empowered to overcome fear and step into the abundant life He has for us.

**Message of Hope**

To those who are walking through the intense journey of labor and childbirth, remember you are not alone. God sees your pain, He understands your fears, and He is with you every step of the way. In the midst of the struggle, there is a promise of new life, and that life is a gift from God—a testament to His faithfulness and His creative power.

The process may seem overwhelming, filled with moments of exhaustion and uncertainty, but hold on to the hope that you are bringing forth something beautiful. Just as a seed must be buried and endure the dark and difficult process of growth before it can bloom, your efforts and pain will bear fruit. The challenges you face are not in vain, and you are not defined by the difficulty of the moment, but by the strength that God gives you to endure.

In the midst of your struggle, trust that God is with you, guiding you, comforting you, and strengthening you. The Bible tells us in Isaiah 41:10, *"Do not fear, for I am with you; do not be dismayed, for I am your God. I will strengthen you and help you; I will uphold you with my righteous right hand."* He has equipped you for this moment, and His grace is sufficient to carry you through.

Though labor is intense, there is a joy that comes with it—the joy of bringing life into the world, the joy of witnessing God's miracle in your own body. Keep your eyes on the prize, knowing you will hold your precious child in your arms, and in that moment, the struggle will fade away into the beauty of new beginnings.

Take heart, for God is your strength, and He will carry you through this. You are stronger than you realize, and His peace will sustain you. Trust that this journey, though difficult, will bring you to a place of joy and fulfillment. Your labor is not in vain, and the hope that lies ahead is worth every moment of struggle. You are surrounded by God's love, and He will see you through to victory.

**Declarations**

I declare that I am strong, courageous and capable, empowered by the grace and strength of God to bring forth new life. As I approach the moment of giving birth, I trust that the Lord is with me, guiding me through every contraction, every moment of discomfort, and every challenge I may face. I declare I will experience peace in the midst of the storm, knowing God is in control and His perfect plan is unfolding in my life.

I declare my body is designed and equipped by God to carry and deliver this child with strength, endurance and ease. I release all fear, anxiety and worry, and I place my trust in God's timing and His protection over my child and me. I declare my body will respond to labor with calmness and confidence, and every part of this process will be smooth and safe, according to God's will.

I declare I will experience no harm, no complications, and no fear as I give birth. My child will be born healthy, strong, and full of life. I trust that God will surround me with a supportive team and His presence will fill the room, bringing peace, comfort and protection. I declare this birth will be a testimony to God's faithfulness and love, and that the joy of bringing this child into the world will outweigh any pain or struggle.

I declare I am fully equipped to embrace motherhood, and I will walk in the strength and wisdom God provides. This moment is a blessing, and I declare my child's life will be filled with purpose, love, and the guidance of the Holy Spirit. I give thanks to God for His grace, protection, and for the miracle of new life.

# Testimony #8
## Embracing Education as a Calling

**Jeremiah 29:11 KJV**
*"For I know the thoughts that I think toward you, saith the LORD, thoughts of peace, and not of evil, to give you an expected end."*

Growing up, I was always told education was the key to success, and I knew it was important. But deep down, I could not stand school. The problem was not my capability. On the contrary, I excelled academically with ease. But, I was disinterested. I wanted to have fun, experience life in ways that did not involve textbooks or exams. The structured environment of school felt restrictive to me. I never had the desire to finish high school, let alone think about higher education. My focus was on what was immediately enjoyable, not on the long-term goals that education could provide.

However, despite my reluctance, I somehow found myself graduating from high school. It was not out of passion or ambition, but rather a sense of obligation to get through it. After high school, I decided to take the next step and enroll in college. To my surprise, I ended up in an undergraduate psychology program. I was not passionate about the subject at first, but over time, I realized psychology offered a fascinating insight into the human mind and behavior. I graduated with a Bachelor of Science in Psychology, an accomplishment that was hard to ignore. But I was still unclear about what to do next with my education or career.

**Taking a Break – The Year of Reflection**

After graduation, I took a year off. I was exhausted from the pressure of school and unsure of the direction I wanted to go. The idea of continuing my education felt like a heavy burden, and I was not sure what job I wanted to pursue. I was in a place of confusion, still craving freedom and the joy of life that was not tied to academic pursuits.

But God had a plan for me, even though I could not see it at the time. One day, I received a word from God, and it was confirmed through my apostle. I felt a strong pull to continue my education, to push beyond my comfort zone, and to go further. It was not just a call for the sake of success or a career. God was telling me He had more for me—more than I had imagined. It was time to go further in my education, and He wanted me to pursue a higher calling.

**The Master's Journey – Answering the Call**

I listened to that call and enrolled in a master's program in school counseling. Initially, I still questioned whether I had made the right choice, but as the program progressed, I began to feel a sense of purpose. I realized I had been equipped with knowledge and insight that could truly help others. School counseling was a natural extension of what I had studied in psychology, and the more I learned, the more I saw God's hand guiding me in the process.

But this was not the end of my educational journey. Toward the end of my master's program, God spoke to me once again. He told me I was to pursue a doctorate. I was hesitant at first. Did I really want to go that far? But in prayer, I received confirmation. The LORD made it clear that my next step was to pursue a doctorate in pastoral counseling. The idea of adding *doctor* to my name felt both exciting and daunting, but I knew this was part of God's plan for my life. He was calling me to go deeper, to not only help others through counseling but to do so in a way that aligned with His will.

**The Battle Before Victory – The Enemy's Resistance**

The journey to my doctorate was not easy. As I worked on my dissertation, I faced opposition like I had never experienced before. The enemy fought relentlessly against me. Every step forward seemed to be met with delays, distractions and discouragement. There were times when I wondered if I would ever finish. The pressure was overwhelming, and I found myself questioning whether I could truly overcome the obstacles that stood in my way.

But God, in His faithfulness, did not leave me to face this battle alone. One night, during a time of prayer, I had a dream that revealed the spiritual battle I was facing. In the dream, I saw the enemy working hard to prevent me from completing my dissertation. But God did not leave me in despair. He also showed me the end result. He revealed to me that I would finish. It was as if God was lifting my eyes beyond the present struggle and giving me a glimpse of the victory ahead.

This dream reignited my faith. I knew I had to press on, even though the enemy was fighting against me. I called on my support system - my husband, my dad, and my apostle - and together, we prayed. We prayed for breakthrough, for strength, and for God's will to be done. Within two weeks of giving birth to my second child, I received the incredible news - I had officially completed my dissertation, and I had become a doctor.

**A Moment of Triumph – God's Perfect Timing**

I could not believe it. I had done it. The years of hard work, the battles fought, the tears, the doubts—it was all worth it. And to top it all off, God had orchestrated this achievement in His perfect timing. Two weeks after the birth of my second child, I had my doctorate. It felt like a supernatural act, a sign of God's faithfulness, and His divine timing in my life.

Looking back, I see how God was with me through every step of the journey. There were times when I did not think I could go on, times when I questioned whether I was truly capable. But every step of the way, He reminded me that He had called me, equipped me, and was with me in the process. My education journey was not just about degrees and titles. It was about my obedience to God's calling on my life and trusting He would make a way when there seemed to be no way.

**The Faithfulness of God**

The journey from being reluctant to becoming a doctor was not an easy one, but it was a testament to God's faithfulness. He took me from a place of indifference to a place of purpose. He showed me that even when I do not have the answers, He does. Through every delay, every struggle, and every prayer, God showed me His hand at work in my life.

If you are on a similar journey - whether it is in education, career, or calling – remember God has a plan for you. It may not always be easy, and it may not look like what you envisioned, but trust that He is faithful to see you through to the end. Keep pressing forward. Trust Him in the struggle. And remember His timing is always perfect. You may face delays and opposition, but with God, you will always reach the victory He has promised you.

**No Limitations: I CAN**

The LORD spoke to me and said, *"We limit ourselves because of two words: I CAN'T!"* These words, though small, carry great weight. They become barriers to your potential, shackling you to a mindset that limits what God can do in your life. The enemy thrives on keeping you stuck in this mindset, perpetually whispering *"I can't"* in your ear. But, it is time to silence those *"I can'ts"* and declare your *"I CANS!"* It is time to stand up and speak life into your situation, because the power of life and death is in your words.

Proverbs 18:21 (KJV) says, *"Death and life are in the power of the tongue: and they that love it shall eat the fruit thereof."* Your *"I can't"* represents death because it kills your purpose and robs you of the dreams God has placed in your heart. On the other hand, *"I can"* represents life, for it pushes you to birth your purpose and walk boldly into the destiny God has prepared for you.

Where do these words come from? The words we speak are born in our minds, shaped by our thoughts. If we continually tell ourselves, *"I can't,"* we are reinforcing a mindset that limits us. But when we shift our thinking and begin to speak what God says about us, we open ourselves to the limitless possibilities He has for our lives.

**Fixed Mindset vs. Growth Mindset**

In psychology, there is a concept known as the *fixed mindset* vs. *growth mindset* introduced by psychologist Carol Dweck. This concept helps us understand why some people are able to overcome challenges and others get stuck in defeat. Which category do you think *"I can't"* falls under? Is it fixed or growth?

In Proverbs 23:7, it says, *"For as he thinketh in his heart, so is he."* Our thoughts shape our actions and determine the direction of our lives. When we have a fixed mindset, we believe our abilities, intelligence and talents are static, making us unable to grow or improve. This mindset traps us in a cycle of *"I can't."* It makes us doubt our potential and keeps us comfortable, preventing us from stepping into the fullness of what God has for us.

On the other hand, a growth mindset believes that with effort, learning, and persistence, our abilities can grow. *"I can"* becomes the driving force, propelling us forward to new heights. A growth mindset opens the door for progress and change, allowing us to see challenges as opportunities for growth. When we think we can, we take the necessary steps to improve and stretch ourselves. It is not about being perfect, but about making progress.

The mind and body are connected. What we think influences how we act. If we believe we cannot, our actions will align with that belief, and we will remain stagnant. But when we believe we can, we take steps to grow, we pursue opportunities, and we overcome obstacles.

**Breaking the Yoke of "I Can't"**

Just like the prophet Isaiah speaks about breaking the yoke of oppression, many of us are carrying the yoke of *"I can't."* This yoke weighs us down, restricting us from moving forward into the fullness of what God has called us to do.

**Isaiah 58:6** says, *"Is not this the fast that I have chosen? to loose the bands of wickedness, to undo the heavy burdens, and to let the oppressed go free, and that ye break every yoke?"* The yoke of *"I can't"* is a heavy burden. It holds you back from your God-given purpose. God wants to break that yoke off your life and set you free to walk in His calling.

When we declare *"I can"* and believe it in our hearts, we are breaking the chains of limitation. We are choosing to step out of the box and into the limitless possibilities that God has for us.

**God's Response to "I Can't"**

God's response to our *"I can't"* is found in Philippians 4:13 (KJV), which says, *"I can do all things through Christ which strengtheneth me."* If we limit ourselves, we are limiting God, because He is the One who gives us strength. He has equipped us with everything we need to accomplish His will on earth. When we say *"I can't,"* we are denying His power and His ability to work through us.

**Have a Growth Mindset**

To overcome the *"I can't"* mentality, we must cultivate a growth mindset. This means actively pursuing growth opportunities. It means attending conferences, joining Bible studies, volunteering, and seeking out a spiritual mentor. Do not shy away from challenges. See them as opportunities from God to grow in faith, knowledge and purpose.

The disciples in the book of Acts had a growth mindset. They believed that waiting on God would lead to growth, and as a result, the Holy Spirit filled them, and they preached boldly. They took the challenge to go and make disciples seriously, and God worked through them in mighty ways. They had no limitations in their thinking, and God moved mightily through them.

## What's Causing Me to Limit Myself?

Ask yourself, what's causing you to limit yourself and God? Is it fear of failure, fear of rejection, self-doubt, comparison to others, or labels from the past? Maybe it is a lack of vision or a comfort zone that you do not want to step out of. Whatever it is, it is time to address it and stop allowing these things to hold you back from God's calling on your life.

## Stop Avoiding What God Wants to Use

Stop avoiding the very thing God wants to use to fulfill His purpose in your life. You may think you are not qualified or capable, but God does not call the qualified, He qualifies the called. Step out in faith and declare that with God, you can do all things.

Many of you have been saying, *"I can't"* in different areas of your life. Let us change that narrative:

- "I can't preach." – Yes, you can, with God's help.
- "I can't bless others." – Yes, you can, no matter your financial situation.
- "I can't start that business." – Yes, you can. God will provide.
- "I can't be a witness." – Yes, you can. God will give you the words.
- "I can't be healed." – Yes, you can. By His stripes, you are healed.
- "I can't overcome this addiction." – Yes, you can, through His strength.
- "I can't get that promotion." – Yes, you can. Favor is on your side.
- "I can't improve my marriage." – Yes, you can, with God's love and grace.

**Speak Over Your Life**

Today, let us declare we are no longer limited by the words *"I can't."* Speak life into every area of your life and declare:

- "I can do all things through Christ who strengthens me."
- "I can overcome every obstacle in my path."
- "I can fulfill God's purpose for my life."
- "I can walk in the freedom God has for me."

**Spirit of Failure**

The spirit of failure is not just about struggling with grades or facing setbacks—it is a mindset and a spiritual attack that seeks to make a person feel inadequate and incapable of succeeding. It is an oppressive force that often strikes when someone is on the brink of personal or academic achievement. The enemy understands that education is not just about acquiring knowledge. It is a means through which people can rise above their circumstances, change their lives, and make a positive difference in the world. Therefore, the spirit of failure targets students, particularly those who are trying to build their lives through learning and growth.

This spirit manifests as thoughts of inadequacy, fear of failure, and a belief that success is impossible or out of reach. It whispers lies like, *"You're not smart enough," "You'll never be able to make it,"* or *"You don't have what it takes."* These doubts can cripple a person's sense of self-worth and prevent them from putting in the effort or taking the necessary steps to succeed.

**Overcoming the Spirit of Failure**

The good news is that you do not have to be controlled by the spirit of failure. By recognizing its tactics, you can begin to resist its influence and step into the success and fulfillment that God has prepared for you. Here are several steps to overcome the spirit of failure:

1. **Renew Your Mind with Truth**: The first step in overcoming failure is renewing your mind with the truth of God's Word. When the spirit of failure whispers lies of inadequacy and fear, respond with Scripture that reminds you of who you are in Christ. God has equipped you with everything you need to succeed (2 Peter 1:3). He has not given you a spirit of fear but of power, love, and a sound mind (2 Timothy 1:7).

2. **Embrace Failure as a Learning Opportunity**: Instead of seeing failure as the end, view it as a lesson that helps you grow. Every mistake is an opportunity to learn, improve, and become more resilient. Recognize that success is built on a foundation of perseverance, and failure is just part of that process.

3. **Focus on Progress, Not Perfection**: Let go of perfectionism and focus on progress. Celebrate the small victories, whether it is completing a difficult assignment or simply staying focused during a study session. Trust that God is working through you, and take each step forward with faith and determination.

4. **Seek Support from Others**: Do not isolate yourself when you struggle. Surround yourself with supportive friends, mentors and educators who can encourage you and help you keep a positive perspective. Talking about your fears and doubts with others can break the power of the spirit of failure and help you see things more clearly.

5. **Pray for Strength and Guidance**: Pray for strength and wisdom to navigate the challenges you face in education. Ask God to help you overcome any fear, doubt or discouragement and to equip you with the perseverance and focus you need. When you invite God into your academic journey, you tap into a power greater than yourself.

The spirit of failure is a deceptive and destructive force that seeks to rob you of your potential and keep you from succeeding in education. However, as a believer in Christ, you have the power to overcome this spirit. By renewing your mind with the truth of God's Word, embracing failure as a stepping stone, and focusing on progress rather than perfection, you can break free from the spirit of failure. Trust that with God's help, you can succeed in your education and step into the future He has prepared for you. Your academic journey is not about avoiding failure but about growing through it, learning from it, and ultimately succeeding with God's guidance and strength.

**Message of Hope**

To those feeling weary or discouraged as you near the end of your school journey, know that hope is within reach. The path you have walked, though challenging at times, has prepared you for what is to come. Remember that every test, every late night of studying, and every moment of struggle has shaped you into someone who is stronger and more resilient than you realize.

You are not alone in this. God is with you, guiding your steps and providing the strength you need to finish strong. Philippians 4:13 reminds us, *"I can do all things through Christ who strengthens me."* Even when it feels difficult, His strength is more than enough to carry you through to the finish line. Do not give up because you are closer than you think.

Take a deep breath and trust in God's perfect timing. He has brought you this far, and He will see you through to the end. The finish line is in sight, and on the other side, there are new opportunities, new beginnings, and greater purpose waiting for you. Keep pushing, one step at a time. You are capable, you are worthy, and you are ready to finish what you started.

As you keep going, remember that hope is your anchor, and God's plans for you are far greater than you can imagine. You are equipped, you are strong, and your perseverance will lead you to victory. The best is yet to come. Finish strong, knowing the rewards of your hard work are on the horizon!

I declare that I am walking in God's purpose and plan for my life as I continue my education. I trust in His wisdom and guidance, knowing that He is with me every step of the way. I am equipped with the strength, knowledge, and perseverance needed to finish my studies successfully.

No challenge or obstacle will stand in my way, for I am more than a conqueror through Christ. I declare that I am blessed with a sound mind, clarity of thought, and the ability to learn quickly. My work is not in vain, for God has a purpose for every assignment I complete.

**Declarations**

I declare I will finish this season of my life with excellence, humility and grace. God's favor surrounds me, opening doors of opportunity and success. I will not be discouraged by setbacks, but will continue to trust in His perfect timing and provision.

I am more than capable, because I rely on God's strength, not my own. I declare I will finish my schooling with joy, peace and fulfillment, knowing that all things work together for my good according to God's will.

**Write it Down!**

I encourage you to write down your testimonies. Take the time to reflect on the moments in your life where God has moved mightily. Whether it was through healing, provision, deliverance, breakthrough, or simply His presence guiding you, each testimony is a powerful reminder of His faithfulness and love.

Your story is unique, and it holds the power to impact others in ways you may not even realize. God has given you a testimony—a story not just for you but for those around you. You may think your testimony is not significant or that it is too small, but remember, God uses all things for His glory. Sometimes the simplest story is the one that speaks the loudest to someone in need.

Sharing your testimony with others can encourage, uplift, and bring hope to someone who is struggling. Your story could be the very thing that leads someone to Christ or helps them through a difficult season. God has used your journey, your struggles, and your victories to shape you and give you wisdom that can bring light to others.

I urge you to take the time to write down your experiences and reflect on how God has worked in your life. Then, do not keep it to yourself. Share it with those around you. Whether through conversation, writing, or even a simple post on social media, your testimony could be the encouragement someone desperately needs. You may never know the full impact of your words, but trust that God will use your testimony in ways you cannot see.

Remember, every testimony, no matter how big or small, is a testament to God's goodness. Your story matters, and God will use it to touch lives in powerful ways. So, write it down, share it, and watch as God moves through your obedience to share His work in your life.

**My Testimonies**

### 1. Testimony of Salvation
*How I Came to Know Christ:*

### 2. Testimony of Healing
*Physical or Emotional Healing:*

### 3. Testimony of Provision
*God's Faithfulness in Providing:*

### 4. Testimony of Deliverance
*Freedom from Strongholds:*

## 5. Testimony of Breakthrough
*Overcoming Obstacles:*




## 6. Testimony of Calling and Purpose
*God's Direction in My Life:*




## 7. Testimony of Spiritual Growth
*Transforming My Walk with God:*




## 8. Testimony of Miracles and Wonders
*Experiences of the Supernatural:*

# ACKNOWLEDGMENTS

First and foremost, I give all honor and thanks to my LORD and Savior, Jesus Christ. Every testimony written here is proof of Your healing, delivering, and sustaining power. Without You, none of this would have been possible. To You be all the glory.

To my loving husband, Keith A. Burgess, and to our precious children—thank you for your unconditional love, patience, and constant encouragement. You believed in me when I questioned myself and lifted me up when the journey felt overwhelming. Your faith in me, your prayers, and your unwavering support gave me the strength to keep going and reminded me of God's faithfulness every step of the way. I am deeply grateful to share this journey with each of you.

To my father, Hazrat A. Lalmohamed—thank you for instilling in me the values of hard work, integrity and perseverance, and for raising me on the firm foundation of God's word. Your prayers, guidance, and unwavering faith have shaped my character and provided the spiritual strength that continues to sustain me. The lessons you taught me have been the cornerstone of my success and a guiding light in every season of my life.

To Apostle Paul and Pastor Norma Mangroo—your spiritual covering, prayers and encouragement have been a great blessing to my life. Thank you for pouring into me, believing in me, and reminding me to keep pressing forward in the things of God.

To my professors at Liberty University—thank you for imparting knowledge, wisdom and discipline that challenged me to grow, not only academically but also spiritually and personally. Your guidance has helped shape me into the writer and counselor I am today.

To my extended family, friends, mentors, and church family— thank you for your love, prayers and support throughout this journey. Every word of encouragement, every prayer, and every act of kindness pushed me closer to the finish line.

And finally, to every reader of this book: thank you for allowing me to share my testimony with you. My prayer is that through these pages, you will encounter the healing, deliverance and freedom that only Jesus Christ can give.

# ABOUT THE AUTHOR

Dr. Rebecca Burgess is a passionate author and counselor with a Doctorate in Pastoral Counseling. With years of experience helping individuals navigate through emotional and spiritual challenges, Dr. Burgess is dedicated to guiding others toward healing, restoration, and a deeper relationship with God. Through her own personal journey of faith, healing and deliverance, she has experienced firsthand the transformative power of God's love and grace. Dr. Burgess' writing is rooted in biblical truth and personal testimony, offering practical wisdom and encouragement to those who are struggling with life's difficulties. She believes that through Christ, all things are possible, and her mission is to help others find hope, healing and breakthrough with the power of the Holy Spirit.

**Stay Connected!**

 **dr.rebeccaburgess**

 **DrRebeccaBurgess**